SELECTED TWEETS

SELECTED TWEETS
TAO LIN

Short Flight / Long Drive Books
a division of HOBART Publishing

SHORT FLIGHT / LONG DRIVE BOOKS
a division of HOBART
PO Box 1658
Ann Arbor, MI 48106
www.hobartpulp.com/minibooks

These were originally published on Twitter, sometimes in slightly different form.

ISBN: 978-0-9896950-2-2

Printed in the United States of America

Inside text set in Georgia
Illustrations by Mira Gonzalez

SELECTED TWEETS

EXTRAS

2008

August

eating watermelon

editing second novel

opened my door on way out of my room and sort of looked down and felt something like 'really happy' for ~1/3 of a second

November

made a small, neutral-sounding noise with no discernible function alone in my room in the dark on my bed

deleted all 'angelica kitchen' and 'fighting with brother' scenes from novella, focus is now completely on failed shoplifting/relationships

December

sitting in fetal position on chair staring at computer thinking 'what should i eat'

held a pot toward my face to smell it for some reason and hit my face by accident

2009

January

felt an urge to change my blog name to a cliché like 'the double-edged sword' or 'the cup is half empty' or 'the cream of the crop'

March

lying in darkness under blanket holding pillow with neutral facial expression thinking 'neutral facial expression'

April

excitedly thought about writing a story called 'the "unreliable piece of shit" giant squid' ~3 nights ago, still feel excited about it

ate probably 1200+ calories of raw organic cheese, raw organic almonds, raw organic cashews

May

tried to rip a lemon in half, seemed like it was working but when i looked at the lemon it was the same

should i become the complete opposite of who i am now 'for something to do'

thought 'what is beer battered shrimp' in a severely depressed monotone while walking toward my bed after seeing no messages on phone

June

suddenly thought 'aretha franklin' while staring at cauliflower and broccoli being boiled

July

feel like i'm going to shrivel in a 2-3-second process into something 1" x 2" that people will assume is a dehydrated baby carrot

October

felt the possibility of enjoyably blogging quirky, humorous summaries of 10-15 ann beattie short stories 'enter me' and 'disintegrate' feel like masturbating by rubbing pasta on my crotch while somehow eating the pasta with my crotch

November

person next to me in computer lab is bidding on ~$3.5k minivan on ebay, has 'strategies for bidding' opened, is staring tensely at screen

December

'bringing in the new year' reading blake bailey's john cheever biography on my bed near my space heater, nursing a smoothie

2010

January

bought used 1979 paperback of ann beattie's 'distortions' in thrift store for $1 and there was a 1969 $100 bill inside

dreamed i went to jail for shoplifting and many inmates were grinning because they were tweeting a lot i think i keep scratching myself using unnecessarily ape-like positions in terms of my elbow's angle/direction

washed a cup and wrapped it with paper towel and felt like i was wrapping a baby [cute animal] in a blanket and felt emotional

have typed variations of 'how did my life come to this...' ~4 times in past ~20 hours in email, gmail chat, and maybe facebook chat

March

felt a kind of tenderness or humanity toward my oranges as i was handling them in the making of a smoothie, seemed bleak

opened an opti-free contact lenses solution box and tenderly held the 10 ounce bottle with both hands and thought it seemed small

middle-aged, suited, caucasian man sneezed making a noise like a baby demon 'screaming in agony' then said 'excuse me' in a normal voice

April

answering emails with a strong/sustained sensation of low-level faux-pas and an intermittent 'strong fear' of major faux-pas

simultaneously thought 'what is...happening' and 'what the...hell...is this' in a continuous, detached manner while badly peeling an orange

created a 10-ingredient salad (kale, cucumber, onion, garlic, alfalfa sprouts, wakame, arame, flaxseed oil, tamari, lime juice)

May

vaguely thought 'why is this my life' in the manner one might think 'why is there no stop sign at this intersection' while looking at a cat

about to idly rewatch 'go' on hulu while eating 4x mango, feeling worried about this for some reason, as if it were a social situation

June

quickly suppressed a '100% friendly, i felt' urge on the r train to help a man fanning himself with his hand by fanning him with my hand

July

person in library glanced at me conspiratorially, feel like i'm involved in a plot to do something but have completely forgotten everything

editing my internet presence in what feels like an arbitrary manner with a sensation of faking a professional facial expression

jamaican woman in 'best buy' said 'i can't carry this heavy ass shit around' while dropping one side of an ipad ~2 inches onto table

August

feel like i have a craving satiable only by [nonexistent activity combining 'idly masturbating'/'eating cold carbs'/'screaming loudly']

thought 'confirm your selection' on movietickets. com was 'confirm your religion' and felt ready to choose 'christian' to 'get past' it

created an alfalfa-mesclun-lacinato kale-nori-dulse-chia seed-garlic-ginger-turmeric-cayenne-raw honey-flax/hemp oil-lemon juice-olive salad

felt an earnest desire to wear earphones that combined qualities of earmuffs/bodybags to enclose my entire head at all times

September

maneuvered through an unruly, unidirectional crowd by repeatedly moving my body in small, weird, self-conscious, robot-like ways

keep imagining myself exiting 'whole foods' and seeing a gigantic billboard in the distance that says 'seems bleak' in neon colors

considered .2-.4 seconds saying 'bless you' to girl ~10 feet away and facing opposite direction in café who sneezed to 'flirt' with her

October

thought 'my life isn't anything...' in a parodically 'emo' tone then 'my life does not seem to be anything...' in a formal/professional tone

thought 'i derive joy from looking at people's faces and thinking "what the hell/fuck am i looking at..."...' while searching for a cafe felt a mild urge to scream 'i don't know what i'm going to eat' in an extremely loud, completely out-of-control, cathartic manner

felt fleetingly endeared to myself upon calmly accepting with shy reluctance that walking to the l train was probably going to feel bleak

felt myself automatically beginning to consider/'plan out' moving to belgrade upon seeing someone from belgrade friended me on facebook

November

think i tried to write the word 'get' by using only one letter and felt confused when it seemed impossible

belligerently thought 'garner, milk, garner, milk' while squeezing/'molding' my head with both hands in 'best buy' at ~5am

repeatedly demonstrated jesse eisenberg-like mannerisms while grinning with unfocused eyes and saying 'jesse eisenberg, do you know him'

December

feels like the entirety of my existence has been masturbating while ~15% erect for ~40 minutes with no foreseeable results

earnestly yelled 'i tweeted...can you look at it...to see if it's okay' in a nearly idle manner from inside bathroom to person 2 rooms away

said 'it gets better with rereadings' re [previous tweet] while petting the shoulder of the person i was addressing and grinning

said 'jesus...i didn't know your eyes were dry' in a vaguely earnest manner after reading [draft of tweet by person sitting to my right]

deleted [draft of a tweet] and typed [tweet you're currently reading] in a businesslike manner after saying 'i'm about to tweet a good one'

pulled my penis in opposite directions near its 'head' to make it wider as @meganboyle poured cocaine on the now-larger surface.

became fixated on refining the idea of an orca taking a bath while staring at different areas of [30' x 80' section of a 'food court']

for ~4 seconds felt myself becoming rapidly convinced, to a degree that i almost felt it as an indisputable truth, that mel gibson is mexican

2011

January

briefly/'somewhat grimly' became aware of a portion of my consciousness where ~80% was monitoring ~20% for tweetable thoughts/feelings

while thinking [what seemed to be 'nothing'] calmly imagined my brain hovering in the distance in a quiet, futuristic setting

seemed to feel 'the same' before/after seemingly successfully convincing myself that if i get everything i want i'll feel 'the same'

while moving cursor to other side of screen experienced a sensation like i was tiredly swinging a shovel across an open area of space

earnestly thought 'what am i supposed to be doing with my life' while multitasking 3-5 long-term
projects with a zombielike expression

thought 'life is not worth living if i care about my
reputation' in a 'braveheart'-esque tone while
mentally drafting email reply to my mom

February

briefly felt like i felt what the girl felt at the end of
'welcome to the dollhouse' while listening to 'sun-
ny day real estate' on a megabus

megabus driver said we're 5 minutes away and i
grimly suppressed an urge to scream 'woohaaaa!'
repeatedly while 'hitting' people

said 'facebook' twice in a 'haunting' voice while
staring at my twitter account with nearly unfocused eyes

from a notably large abstract distance noticed
myself urgently thinking 'i want to feel emotional'
while scrolling through songs on iphone

reacted to a nonsequitur image of myself standing
in parents' house's backyard in sunlight in ~1999

by 'renewing' my zombielike expression

March

does a society exist where it's become acceptable to wear 'helmets' enclosing one's entire head when in public to preempt social interaction

feel like i only want to convey powerful, convincing, unceasing messages of 'i don't know' and 'i have nothing to say to you'

the driver of the boltbus i'm on from nyc to baltimore has been arrested for drunk driving ~2 hours after we left nyc

someone said a 'happy hour' joke and everyone laughed, another person loudly referred to the arresting officer as 'the po po'

person who called 911 has a 'book culture' totebag and said 'i saved your life' angrily while trying to get 1 of 8 seats on 1st 'rescue'-bus

thought 'my eyes are bulging out of my head' while staring at computer screen with an uncontrollable-seeming sensation of sarcastic disbelief gradually began to feel like i existed solely as a hardened sausage while thinking 'i can't do anything' in a continuous, laser-like manner

looked away and mumbled 'i didn't articulate it well...more like a rubbery sausage...' upon being complimented on [previous tweet]

felt an urge to convey to someone that a machine that can sense and instantly produce the exact song you want to hear will likely never exist

thought 'kombucha' in an unexpectedly 'extreme, low-pitched' monotone and imagined an elephant spraying kombucha at me using its trunk

since convincing myself that i can very noticeably 'flash' my eyes have been occasionally 'flashing' my eyes privately, almost secretively

April

thought '"siddhartha 2" as a novel and a novel's title seems more iconic than "siddhartha"' while staring at the word 'while' in gmail

my life would be funnier and more interesting to
me if instead of thinking my internal monologue i
heard it as voiceover maybe

calmly stared at 2 ewok-centered, 'time-sensitive,
to some degree' tweet-drafts in my gmail account
with a mild sensation of mismanagement

thought 'i...' ~4 seconds while staring at [2px x
2px area on the scroll bar on the right side of my
firefox window] with ~80% unfocused eyes

finally feeling good after sleeping ~12 hours and
ingesting addy, xanax, percocet, mdma, caffeine,
carbs, codeine, flexeril around people i like

May

stared at ~5'1"/~20-year-old/asian man running
up stairs and sometimes looking behind him at
another asian man, both holding ice cream cones

thought 'this looks different than the other one'
in a literal manner about a movie's trailer in com-
parison to a different movie's trailer

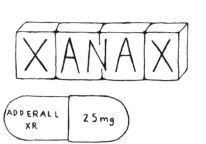

felt increasingly unsure if i already knew about [asteroid named '3412 kafka'] in the minutes after amusedly learning about it on wikipedia

thought 'eyeball tweet' in a manner like i have a pre-existing, successful, beloved gimmick where i tweet about my eyeballs

said 'i feel like if i got brain damage no one would be able to notice' while petting @meganboyle and thinking vaguely about the internet

people who don't know what to title their novels/ movies can title them 'where's waldo' and insert waldo (or not, depending on tone) in one scene

suddenly remembered an ant-based/strategy/ role-playing game i'd forgotten for maybe ~8 years upon seeing 'ulysses s. grant' on a $1 coin*

feel like my urge to 'look at the internet' can be satisfied only by entering the screen with my entire body

thought 'i wish i felt an irrepressible urge to write a surreal, unbroken narrative in ~6 hours non-stop' while feeling a small urge to do that

---

* The game had a character named something like Ulysses S. Ant.

June

felt 'pause' in my expression of myself upon realizing i couldn't photograph my hand holding my
iphone without another iphone

discerned my ~60%-eaten 'haitian mango' as
'sopping wet' and felt a 'vague, as-yet unresolved'
interest in its inanimately sopping nature

seemed to earnestly resent [person to my left] in
computer lab for sitting by me despite me having
been the person to sit by them...

imagined postponing someone's suicide by convincing them to instead 'get as many people as
possible to speak with an irish accent'

imagined a 'kobo abe*-esque' scenario where i'm
forced to devote my life to creating facebook2
where people's screens can be viewed in real-time

@nytyrant i'm in the laguardia airport food court,
look behind you

---

* Author of *The Woman in the Dunes* (1962),*The Box Man* (1973), and other
novels.

@nytyrant i see you, walking over to you now

@nytyrant just kidding, i'm in my bed

someone in my row seems to be hissing sometimes #xmenlivetweet[*]

i can hear someone snoring from ~8 seats to my left #xmenlivetweet

someone seems to be laying across 2 seats sleeping #xmenlivetweet

somehow felt an epiphany-like premonition that when i'm 29 my life will be exactly like what it will be like when i'm 29

absently rubbed my extremely limp penis while chewing coconut meat and staring with 60% unfocused eyes at the word 'chicken' in gmail chat

---

[*] *X-Men: First Class* (2011) is a superhero film set "primarily in 1962 during the Cuban Missile Crisis" (Wikipedia).

woman outside bobst library[*] said 'oh, they killed themselves inside?' in an ultimately unilluminating, 'dawning realization'-like manner

asked someone a yes/no question and he talked for ~30 seconds until i walked meekly away #boltbusdelaylivetweet[**]

people seem to be deriving joy from anti-delay camaraderie that is stronger than delay disappointment #boltbusdelaylivetweet

blind woman hit me with walking stick ~2 seconds after someone said 'there's a blind woman' in warning #boltbusdelaylivetweet

heard '831, 831' in a 'star wars'-esque voice re [bus 0831], 19 minutes into delay #boltbusdelaylivetweet

boarded [bus 0831], felt momentarily confused why/how 2 different people are 'both' wearing green shirts #boltbusdelaylivetweet

---

[*] NYU's 12-floor library. "In late 2003, the library was the site of two suicides. In separate incidents, students jumped from the open-air crosswalks inside the library and fell to the stereogram-patterned marble floor below " (Wikipedia)

[**] There was a delay for the bus from Manhattan to Baltimore.

imagined mark ruffalo feeding jim carrey xanax through his 'pee hole' as part of the memory-erasure process #eslivetweet*

imagined a version of this where 'inspector gadget' repeatedly tries to erase the memory of himself #eslivetweet

thought 'is jim carrey a catfish?' while trying to 'figure out' jim carrey #eslivetweet

felt like jim carrey is a velociraptor that, incredibly, beyond all expectations, has succeeded as a human actor/comedian #eslivetweet

imagined jim carrey nonsequiturly punching kate winslet in the face really hard in a misguided attempt at zaniness #eslivetweet

imagined nicolas cage trying to convince the director to let him improvise a scene where he frugally cuts his hair with fire #swlivetweet**

---

* *Eternal Sunshine of the Spotless Mind* (2004) is a movie written by Charlie Kaufman.

** *Season of the Witch* (2001) is a "fantasy adventure horror " (Wikipedia) starring Nicolas Cage.

someone said 'this is a grave' then in a manner like he had misremembered his line said 'this is a mass grave' #swlivetweet

the hispanic-looking 'page' seems like he isn't trying to act at all, to a degree that seems shocking... #swlivetweet

nicolas cage has been saying a word that sounds like 'prozac' to refer to the priest #swlivetweet

the priest seemed to yell 'ceviche' (the mexican/ seafood dish) during his incantation against the demon-thing #swlivetweet

nicolas cage said 'why would he tie himself to a desk?' in a manner like he was helping edit an early draft of this movie #swlivetweet

the demon-thing is intermittently hitting nicolas cage's backside with the 'wrist' part of one of its wings #swlivetweet

imagined obama accidentally beginning a live/ televised speech with 'few people believe mexicans are funny as much as i do'

science-fiction novel set in a future where the only way to get a computer is to build it yourself and you have to build it before you're 15

July

yearned for someone to carry me on a stretcher to a corner of my room where there would be a cave i could crawl into for comfort

thought something like 'i can't work on my novel in this environment' with 'this environment' referring to [the universe, i think]

imagined a baboon displaying no discernible reaction (or lack of a reaction) after consciously and legitimately 'beating me' in chess

werner herzog should direct a short film in which a baboon is attacked by hundreds of lobsters and dies in a 'succumbing' manner

science-fiction novel in which [sneaking into a middle school and living there for 30 days] has become a meme that is 'crippling' america

it should be legal to commit suicide if you train 5+ years until you're able to rip your head off with your bare hands

felt a medium-strong desire to write an extremely halfassed, unauthorized, internet-researched biography of charlie sheen

australian man in 'whole foods' said variations of 'you want the mango flavor?' 4-8 times in ~10 seconds to his ~2-year-old child

thought 'how many ronald reagans were there...' in a mildly panicked tone then another part of my brain answered '3' curtly/calmly

became aware of myself earnestly considering adopting more of a sleep-based lifestyle, a life in which i'd mostly be sleeping

felt distracted from working on things by [image of me and a chupacabra sitting on my bed, backs against a wall, my arm avuncularly around it]

stared at '4:26' change to '4:27' on iphone screen thinking 'i'm experiencing a parody of time, my perspective on time now has a tone' imagined myself as a stand-up comedian saying 'what if yao ming never played basketball?' then silence except 1 man laughing incredibly hard

August

said 'i haven't tweeted anything...' re [previous ~2 hours of 4+ 'heavily edited, abandoned' tweets] and held my head in a parody of anguish

felt a desire for a grainy, ~8-minute video of schopenhauer interacting with his poodle to exist then felt a desire for it not to exist

macaulay culkin should make 'home alone 5' where he halfassedly organizes his drugs, orders chinese food, and lies facedown on his bed

realized i maybe played tetris on gameboy as an internet-less child in a bleakly 'repeatedly re-freshing websites' manner

felt 'couscous' belligerently try to combine itself to 'consciousness' while repeatedly failing to type 'consciousness' correctly distractedly theorized that life is boring because time cycles in a 24-hour period and there isn't ever an 'extreme' time like 9693:47am

while 'organizing my room' pushed a cardboard box's flap ~4 times up/in and it returned each time to original position

September

became aware of myself intensely 'line editing' my gmail 'tasks list' in service of decreasing enjambment as much as possible

saw my face in bathroom mirror and thought 'spiderman' and 'obese' while imagining inspectah deck sing 'your neighborhood spiderman'

felt unable to stop myself from repeatedly trying to earnestly view 'sci-fi novel in which macbooks can fly' as a 'maybe' for my next book

saw myself belligerently putting my arms around 2 aliens on either side of me (and scared of me) to involve them in my internet experience

felt confident that if i were placed in a roomful of

extraterrestrials i would immediately begin dominating them all conversationally

imagined myself 'idly chasing' a small herd of scared extraterrestrials through a long hallway in an 'american psycho'-esque manner

someone should genetically engineer a peanut plant whose peanuts never stop growing and are larger than earth within ~20 years

felt unsure if i already tweeted [something about wanting to spend the rest of my life convincing as many people as possible that i'm a robot]

feel like i can't stress it enough that i strongly feel that if i'm put in a room with 10+ extraterrestrials i'll easily dominate them all

nightmare situation in which every time i looked at the time i would see that something like 18 hours have passed

thought 'i am going to be a papaya for halloween, i will look exactly like a papaya, no eye-slits, a bus will hit me' in a robotic monotone

my next conscious moment could be me wearing
a ski-mask in a low-lit room staring at 10+ people
i don't recognize tied by rope to chairs

imagined enrolling in a class called 'why to interact with humans' as a 'last resort' and deriving
satisfaction from knowing i won't attend

novel in which kafka lives into his 70s and is
forced by poverty in 1951 to accept a ghostwriting
job on a comprehensive history of ww2

while reading f-16's wikipedia page felt my brain
successfully trying to make me feel afraid of waking in the pilot seat of an airborne f-16

while eating a salad on my bed thought 'should i
talk to her? should i talk to oprah?' in a manner
like she was in the same elevator as me

thought 'darkness descends...descent of darkness...' then 'i want to make video games...but i
don't know' while washing my face

in ~'93 in ~5th grade there was a meme at my
school of throwing things at (or simply hitting)
people and saying 'ricochet'

imagined a world in which i'd currently be smearing 'freezing cold' hummus 'all over' my face in preparation for [i'm not sure what]

felt distracted from the internet by ['eerie' scenario in which i turn my head to someone and say 'something is wrong with my computer screen']

wearing earplugs to look at internet alone in my room due to construction outside window that includes people shouting in a sports-like manner

desiring a form of carbs i feel unable to concretely imagine, something technologically advanced and temperature-less and 'sexy' and clean

became aware of myself earnestly outlining a plan to convince a small group of my friends to commit suicide with me in ~2 years

desiring nachos but mysteriously feel unable to 'pinpoint' the moment(s) in eating them that will cause me to feel the comfort i desire

October

@simonherzog i felt attracted to naming it 'werner herzog' but finally chose 'richard yates' in part because your dad is still alive*

imagined spending the rest of my life trying to convince people that me saying 'what if i titled my novel "curiosity killed the cat"' is funny

occasionally felt the presence of my room as a distinct entity with a magnet-like attraction for me while away from it today

thought 'struggled to discern what to eat...' in preemptive narration of my life while approaching the refrigerator at a normal speed

struggled to imagine a baboon yodeling, succeeded only when i imagined the sound exiting the top of its expressionless-faced head vertically

feels like the computer screen is idly 'attacking

---

* Simon Herzog, one of Werner Herzog's sons, tweeted "Dear @tao_lin: why didn't you name Richard Yates Werner Herzog instead, it would have made me happie #represent #dad pic.twitter.com/RhCblFrp" at 5:12PM. The picture was a screenshot of a comment I made on a blog in which I mention having considered titling *Richard Yates*, my second novel, *Werner Herzog*. I responded to Simon's question at 5:35PM.

me' to entertain itself as i struggle to do things on the internet and in msword

imagined a badly lost, time-traveling cyborg fighting 100+ jellyfish while experiencing 'severe water damage' #timetravelingcyborgproblems

feel like i'm vaguely on some kind of mission to spread a messageless form of information that i feel disinterested in editing to coherence

imagined myself intensely 'cursing out' a pre-k teacher for koala discrimination as my 3-year-old koala quietly cries in an adjacent room

felt distinctly like a brontasaurus-velociraptor hybrid while walking aimlessly in my room

while walking aimlessly in my room became aware, with surprise, that i was holding my penis and looking vertically down 'into' its 'pee hole'

thought 'so [culmination of everything] is why i look at twitter' and snickered insanely while trying to be as quiet as possible*

---

* I was on psilocybin when this happened I think.

created a massive, swamp-like stew containing broccoli, onion, organic ham/egg, garlic, [other things] in a 'cream of broccoli' base

novel in which i'm supine under blankets in darkness telepathically teaching 1000+ students seated in another room what 'afk' means*

self-consciously felt a weak/uncertain sensation of 'safety' in the idea that i'm alone inside of my skull and can always hide there

visualized my internet usage as a single, robot-like, bodiless, slimy tentacle repeatedly touching the computer screen with little dabs

reacted to a quiet 'roaring noise' outside my window by failing to discern how to mentally prepare myself to be decimated by an asteroid

thought 'croissant' or 'croissants' ~150 times in ~3 hours with images of dolphins/porpoises/[me in a croissant-suit]/croissants

---

* I started writing something like this and viewed it as a novel then "a long short story" then "a ~3000-word story" then "a story I don't want to think about anymore." I worked on it for more than a year, maybe 10-30 hours a month. Currently I view it as "a story I haven't thought about in months and dread ever working on again."

felt that life might be a 'really hard' video game, like if i put gold worth $169k in my mouth it would disappear and i would gain +1 life

November

discovered a ~3600-word story by me from college i completely forgot about that begins 'His name was Xorlorke. Pronounced zor-lore-key'

elderly woman on bus stared at me in fear/aversion/confusion/concern as i left/'returned to'/left seat via indecision

imagined a futuristic entity deriving pleasure from continuously eating nachos by having them float repeatedly back/forth between 2 areas

feel like i've finally begun to realize how 'insane' it seems that for millions of years the same kinds of dinosaurs kept living/dying repeatedly

feels like i'm being forced to live and work for minimum wage in a tiny, invisible room at the back of my head as a manager for my mind/body

2-hour movie called 'nonstop eating' in which i
eat for 24 hours (sped-up 12x) while looking at
the internet with narration by werner herzog

typed 'panicking' in gmail chat as follows (con-
secutively): 'pacniking' 'paniacking' 'paniackgin'
'pacniacking' 'pnacinking'

i feel aversion to people in public bathrooms who
openly stare at me with haunted, expectant ex-
pressions while leisurely washing their hands

acronym i feel would be useful to have in existence: ufsi, 'unfit for social interaction,' i.e. 'sorry,
i'm ufsi this week, maybe next week'

almost every time i read 'bacon' or 'waffle[s]' or
'pancake[s]' or 'nachos' on twitter i strongly desire eating [whatever word i read]

became aware of myself trying to discern what i
want to eat by imagining various foods being already inside of me and felt belittled by myself

imagined a murderer in a movie saying 'if i wanted to kill you wouldn't i have already done it by
now?' and the victim feeling mostly confused

absently/repeatedly thought 'nothing to lose' while eating organic spelt ribbons and repeatedly refreshing various websites

December

if i look at something that's above my head and in front of me without moving my neck or head my expression feels distinctly demonic

i want to publish a scientific paper that proves woody allen has (unbeknownst to himself) been on a large dose of mdma his entire life

2-hour movie of me sitting at a table ingesting drugs nonstop while earnestly stressing the entire time that i 'feel nothing'

epic, intentionally unfunny movie set in a dystopia in which all people, even the tyrannical rulers, are mysteriously supine birth to death

non-profit organization that counters shit-talking/misinformation against people too depressed/unmotivated to defend themselves while walking to my desk suddenly felt that the rapper '50 cent' was hiding in my room somewhere for an explainable, non-malicious reason

collaborative twitter-project: x/y/z follow k for 24hrs, x tweets everything k says, y everything k does, z everything z thinks k thinks*

observed both my hands while repeatedly opening them and allowing them to reflexively revert to ~80% closed positions and felt cyborg-like

12-member hip-hop-collective that only releases songs in which all members simultaneously rap in a layered, indecipherable manner

sympathized with a tiny, hard-working part of my consciousness trying to compose rap lyrics to me clicking things on twitter

what if we're all time-traveling to something like 5 days ago, this is just how you time-travel, by living ~30 years of a life

imagined myself crying on my floor wrapped in

---

* I proposed something like this to an art museum that solicited me for project ideas and they chose someone else's proposal.

a giant, warm, blanket-like pancake that i'm also meekly nibbling

feels like i'm in a horror movie but always ~50 feet away from the scary things and therefore experience life as an ominously plotless movie

imagined myself peacefully dying for unknown reasons while organizing a press conference to announce that my forthcoming novel is unreadable

i want to watch a movie in which christian bale of 'american psycho' is constantly saying 'hold on, i'm trying to livetweet this' agitatedly

i want to be 'peaking' on a medium-large dose of [almost anything] at a large party with my macbook tweeting things and looking at the internet

bringing my macbook to a party tonight

ingesting beer and cookies while looking at twitter

imagined an 'insane' samurai on a battlefield slaying 100+ people while screaming 'coconut water' with no one knowing what 'coconut water' is

riding 'cat-toad hybrid'-waves to fame/riches

'cat-toad hybrid' starring tom hanks

what do we actually know about 'cat-toad hybrid'...?

jesse eisenberg has confirmed for 'cat-toad hybrid: reloaded'

'cat-toad hybrid' has respectfully declined an appearance on oprah

folk-punk band called 'cat-toad fucking hybrid'

literary magazine called 'readable' featuring 'stories, essays, poems, and reviews with a slant toward being readable'

after 3.5 sleepless nights cuba gooding jr. has officially passed on portraying 'cat-toad hybrid' in a made-for-tv movie produced by vh1

i keep visualizing butter or cream cheese being spread onto a plain donut with a butter knife

elderly woman at 'whole foods' seemed to observe what i was selecting (bags of frozen banana-pieces) before reaching for the same thing

i want to strangle whomever invented adderall

memoir titled 'worried about me' with author's worried face on cover

any directors want to cast me as a robot in their movie

imagined waking one morning blind and comically trying to maneuver my life normally without telling anyone (not wanting to bother anyone)

team sport in which 10-person teams fall down as many stairs as possible without injuries (injuries = penalties)

walked into branches of a giant, potted, dead-seeming plant on sidewalk while looking at twitter via iphone

addicted to my bed

500-page book that earnestly answers 'how much damage can an amoeba in its lifetime deliberately inflict on a presidential candidacy?'

feel like if i adhered to 'live each day as if it were your last' i would be dead at the end of every day

feel like my mental health would benefit from an apocalyptic event

felt panic i left my macbook somewhere else while staring at its screen

read 'man survives 2 months in car' as 'man survives 2-month car-crash'

feel like i'll still exist after i die but all other things will be different

i want to live in a solar system where 10+ planets are populated

drug overdoses caused by deficient math skills

i want a pet flounder that lives on land

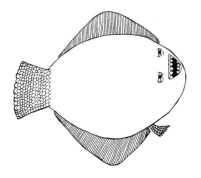

would be convenient if my bed ate me right now

i hope i wake to an alien invasion tomorrow

slept ~8 hours on lsd

thought 'japanese food has an element of... despair'

i see myself standing alone at a low-lit party eating soft carbs in a nonstop manner with a zombie-like demeanor and zero thoughts

thought 'i want to fall thru earth like a neutrino' while looking down at my keys to open my door and seeing the floor in the background

japanese people feel social anxiety in the presence of hummus

nasa should send blobs of hummus into outer space

artificial intelligence will always struggle with the concept of hummus

hummus never appears in hollywood movies, it's too risky

al gore owns 3 tennis rackets made out of only hummus

al gore sometimes daydreams about replacing his neck with hummus

what the hell am i tweeting...

feel like john updike would like my hummus tweets

feel like most people would intuitively go to a pawn shop to buy hummus

imagined a bored 1st-grade-teacher interactively teaching 50+ students how to wash hummus with warm, soapy water before eating it

thought 'i will burn your house down' in a quiet monotone as a nonsequitur while waiting for a site to load

March

what if novels were written by band-like groups
with a person for plot, a person for prose, a person
for themes, a producer, 'mixing,' etc

the more consecutive hours one stays alone in
one's room the larger one's hair becomes (not
only by growing but also 'expanding')

distracted from doing anything because i keep
thinking 'why...am i here...' in reference to both
[the universe] and [specific location]

the inability to discern if the sentences i'm typing are incomprehensible or if my brain currently
can't comprehend comprehensible sentences

brought macbook and childhood blanket to party
last night

emotion called 'i don't want to sleep but i don't
know what i'm waiting for'

a form-fitting layer of internet separates me from
concrete reality

dying by natural causes means you've been down-
loaded in full

lying on bed in darkness wondering what other
people's lives are like

form of martial arts where you train every day for
4 hours without a plan and without remembering
what you did the previous day

believing 'it doesn't matter how much i work on
[unit of art]' while working on it as if it were the
only thing that mattered

moved iphone further away from me on bed, but
still easily within arm's reach, as a strategy to not
push 'snooze' again

imagined 'national geographic'-style narration
'this human is trying to remember what website
he was going to look at' while trying to do that

behind the macbook screen i'm safe from all of
you

basketball team called 'the drug addicts' ('los angeles drug addicts')

basketball team called 'the insomniacs' ('new york
insomniacs')

sci-fi movie in which honey is extremely valuable
and almost every rapper has a song about pouring
tea into honey instead of honey into tea

grinned serenely while thinking 'debbie downer'

nonhumorous movie about a killing rampage in
an urban area on a night when it's okay for drunk
people to be outside idly making loud noises

tylenol pm ad that's a 30-second montage of pat-
rick bateman killing 2-4 people, eating ice cream
at home, ingesting tylenol pm, asleep in bed

imagined myself instantly dying upon exiting my
room into 'outer space' after forgetting i live in a
spaceship that resembles a room

thought 'getting some important retweets from
dick splinter' while seeing that someone called

'dick splinter' was retweeting me

nobel prize category for 'best indian restaurant'

gmail said 'pittsburg' was misspelled and i stared in confusion ~5 seconds before ~40% confidently typing an h between b and u

novel titled 'hiding from nothing alone in my room at 4:44am'

feel 'duly amused' that almost every article re me in print and online is conventionally humiliating and factually incorrect and i think misleading

rapper sponsored by thesaurus.com

April

rapper called 'earplugs' whose brand is that he loves silence

felt affection toward my macbook as it audibly worked, without complaining and like it's happy to help, on converting a file for me

imagined asking random people in williamsburg if they have adderall or xanax and if they do showing them a gun in a subtle, lawful manner

imagined a gorilla doing hilarious stand-up comedy via sign-language

novel with nonsequitur title '4903MJ WL J8094824 09122!@)$ 002948 01294812 AFAL-SKJFAS AFEJF 2091412 LSKJF 2140-I;LJK 240I'

excitedly thought 'stephen hawking should tweet...'

imagined myself grinning at a disinterested passerby while egregiously failing to nurse a tiny, dying tarsier back to life

feel interested in a religion whose main thing is to die of natural causes

imagined someone living a tightly-plotted thriller like 'the bourne supremacy' 80 years nonstop and someone trying to adapt it into a movie

website with pics of insects' detached asses ('bee ass'/'ant ass'/etc) children's book for adults titled 'the missing xanax'

series of books titled 'my opinions' with photo collage of the author on each cover and a standard format (chapters 'on race'/'on gender'/etc)

May

strangers bonding via 'best strangers forever' shirts/hats/etc

dimly remembered using a scottish accent in a dream last night

'xanax olympics' where everyone is tested and must be 'drug free' for 1 year then must ingest 2mg xanax every 4 hours every day of competition

thought 'where be it, where be it' in what sounded like an unknown slang and unknown accent while looking for specific boxer shorts

i will mail my 100,000th follower 150 pounds of things from my room if i become president i'll install tweeting modules in every jail cell, outlaw non-organic farming, [can't think of 3rd thing currently]

~40% certain i've masturbated, as a small child, to bret 'hit man' hart

t-shirt that says 'i survived a ~15%-earnest/ibuprofen suicide-attempt'

what if i found steve jobs hiding under my bed... feel like i really wouldn't know what to do, would either feel scared or, like, annoyed

25-year performance-art project convincing people i got a brain transplant (via documents, video footage, new personality/worldview)

thought of masturbation as 'fucking my penis'

feel like twitter's homepage should be someone walking into tree branches on a college campus while staring at their iphone

recklessly thought 'kicking it into overdrive' while cleaning an area of my bathroom sink in an earnest effort to feel more motivated

self-help book called 'lower your expectations'

song titled 'please throw pills onstage'

1st line of my vampire novel: 'i couldn't remember if my age was ~10,000, ~100,000, or ~100,000,000 and i didn't care'

unintentional elitism via 'no social skills'

embarrassing myself on twitter

retweet if you think 'method man' should change his name to 'cucumber man' every halloween

realized i can pretend i don't speak english in public

change how you think you feel

it is 100% impossible to ruin my life

person playing warcraft 3 next to me in bobst is clicking the mouse incredibly fast, faster than i've ever heard anyone do it

i feel happy for some alienated teenager going home to play diablo 3 after spending time at a family thing

no matter how rich you are the government can always kill you

i want someone to discover me in a dark alleyway crouched naked and whimpering on a major holiday then i want to sprint away suddenly

anthology of 'downward spiral' portions of biographies/autobiographies

TED talks-esque thing where presenters choose a topic at random out of a bag and improvises as if they'd prepared an expert presentation on it

livetweeting this tweet #thistweetlivetweet

stomachdown on my bed like a heavy, paralyzed sea cucumber being slowly absorbed by the sea floor rolled over like a dying, mostly unconscious, beached porpoise or dolphin on my bed away from my macbook clutching a pillow onto my back

reality tv where i go to my followers' homes and thank them for following me, sad episodes where i learn from them that they unfollowed me

imagined a shark swimming through twitter on a vicious rampage attacking people randomly and literally hurting and killing some of us

June

tiny raindrops on a mostly white iphone screen looks pretty

would you squish cats the size of ants? i would feel so scared...

feel like now is the time to express, on twitter, that 'saturday night live' seems very bleak to me and i've always felt alienated by its tone

was sort of shaking my leg in an 'idly tapping' manner when i realized i'm not 100% sure if i saw 'juno'* or not and my leg stopped moving

---

* *Juno* (2007) is a movie starring Ellen Page and Michael Cera.

thought 'i cast aspersions on you' with a strong lisp as a nonsequitur

got an idea...a 24 HOUR PODCAST...think about it

the dalai lama should play himself in a movie where he has somehow become addicted to cantaloupe and actually dies in the movie from this

what if my name was bobo, my parents could've easily done that, thinking it was an uncommon but respectable name

earplugs branded on 'blocking out people' with tagline 'protect your brain from making you feel depressed after hearing people say certain things'

i want to type and look at the internet with only my brain, no hands

i don't think i've been asked in an interview how i want to die, i want to die when a giant star unexpectedly 'plows thru' earth

feel like time began moving way faster for me in 2009

thought about where i actually exist and it feels like i exist on the top/back surface of my left eyeball

searched for my iphone by slowly walking ~3 steps back/forth ~4 times in my room with unfocused eyes thinking 'iphone' and 'where'

stickers that say 'i support the war on america by bath salts'

felt like i was 'lurking' in my own gmail account

you are the president of your own country, the ceo of your own corporation, the editor-in-chief of your own magazine: YOU

July

thought of something...if you implant tiny mirrors into your eyes you could move your peripheral vision in layers into your focused vision

scratched both legs with synchronized move-
ments in time to music

realized i've been privately, idly, sometimes shit-
talking the movie 'whale rider' since seeing ~70%
of it (fell asleep) ~15 years ago

feel like life would make sense if i was the same as
i am now but 15

wish an ex-gf was on twitter

held my glasses thinking they looked different
than before and felt like i was in a horror movie
where someone 'switched out' my glasses

thought 'feminism' absently while touching where
my 'x' button is missing on my macbook

i want my iphone to be more like a pet, to walk
around, etc

feel like if i began a freestyle by saying 'yo' 3-5
times i wouldn't be able to stop saying 'yo', it
wouldn't 'feel right' to stop

cited my journalism degree in email to mom encouraging her to not view 'the media' as an accurate source of information

i want to bring a macbook into batman and try to write a ~40k-word novel during it

openly organized a giant pile of cash in library at computer

'funneled' a liter of cucumber-orange smoothie down my throat

August

i think i remember 0% of pre-calculus

imagined myself saying 'ironically, the novel 1984 actually came out in a year which wasn't the year that that book was called' in a ted talk

thought of my room as a spaceship drifting toward a black hole and felt vaguely, fleetingly different

snickered after thinking 'marimba july' alone in my room

imagined myself getting worried after ~45 minutes that i'm going to die while 'fighting off' a giant turtle repeatedly attacking me in the ocean

felt uncontrollably zany doing mundane tasks alone in my room

i want to fall asleep while laughing quietly

September

nightmare of looking at the ocean feeling terrified

thought 'my glasses god damn it' while on hands and knees

my internal monologue is almost nonstop shit-talking against me

imagined myself strangling someone i've never met while loudly asking 'what is wrong with me?' really wanting to know

what if björk was björnk

imagined a high-level executive saying 'give me a pizza time-frame' instead of 'give me a time-frame' and not realizing the mistake

remembered i had a nightmare in which my hand was in my chest and my childhood toy poodle said 'probably not' as a nonsequitur

i feel like 2012 passed a long time ago, like i remember people being like '2012 passed, world didn't end,' realizing now it's 'still' 2012

obama should wear sunglasses and squint while giving a speech on how he's afraid to close his eyes and afraid to open his eyes

going to start making decisions based on 'what will my future biographer have wanted to be true to write a more readable biography'

imagined myself thinking 'just let me live my shitty life in peace…just let me have this…' while firing fatal shots into people's foreheads

i controlled 2.4% of the dalai lama's conscious thoughts from aug 2 2010 to sep 14 2010 with a computer program on my previous iphone the dalai lama has 48 credit cards and 19 ebay accounts

the dalai lama's favorite 'bright eyes' song is 'nothing gets crossed out'

my iphone feels tiny tonight like it's afraid of me

the dalai lama has a reoccurring nightmare of robocop looking at the internet

sounds like pterodactyls are shrieking outside my window

the computer screen is like a glass wall that is so stained i can't discern what's on the other side but i want to be on the other side

hit my head with my macbook while violent-ly shaking it with both hands to get 'luna bar' crumbs out of the keyboard

berated my brain from a location ~4' behind and ~8' above me

October

feel like i'm functioning in society despite being demon possessed

1 day after turning in novel, life seems incredibly pointless

thought 'shithead' in what felt like an objective tone after cursorily looking at my facebook profile

drifting aimlessly thru whole foods on xanax drinking coconut water listening to dreamily electronic music with earplugs + headphones

the pleasure one gets from eating carbs is so fleeting and obscure compared to, say, being productive while on adderall

feel like no one ever 'eats' anything, the food is just relocated into the stomach from where it was before

in my cold, dark, studio apartment listening to dreamily electronic music

music sounds much better to me the morning after a night of doing things that are harder to linearly remember than normal, i think

realized the reason my room has been 'freaking cold' the past ~40 hours is because my window has been completely open

thought '10 million twitter followers couldn't/wouldn't make me happy' in what vaguely felt like a prideful tone while washing my hands

covered face with both hands in computer lab thinking 'feel...like a misanthropic robot...but misanthropes hate humans...robots...humans'

feel like almost every part of my body is confused about whether what it feels is a desire to pee, orgasm, quietly sob, eat, or sleep

my dad stared blankly at me as i said 'butternut squash' 3 times

my dad referred to chocolate as the 'blackish thing'

my dad said 'female gay'

my dad told me to write 'dog-related poetry'

memoir titled 'skydiving from ground-level to hell'

going back and forth between stores trying to buy an iphone charger while peaking on molly

imagined conor oberst having seizures repeatedly on national tv while struggling to say 'help, i think i'm having a seizure'

everywhere seems like 'inside my room' so far today

i want oprah to say 'i don't understand' to me after a ~5 second pause

said 'i liked talking to xanax' while meaning to say 'i liked talking to david' last night

thought a meek-looking/caucasian man holding a detached bicycle-seat was holding a machine gun in park slope

i keep imagining someone slowly pushing a xanax bar into someone else's eyeball

is any person on earth currently investigating how it came to be (who got the idea, was there a vote, etc) that adderall tastes like candy?

thought 'hurricane intestinal cancer' while closing gmail and standing

would be sweet if a news anchor was like 'use this opportunity to diet/fast, organize your life, clean your room, etc' re hurricane sandy

i can't imagine life after this hurricane, i can't imagine being alive still, i really can't, 2012

eating ice cream with kashi cereal repeatedly poured on top

ingesting .5 ecstasy to help me attain a mental state in which i hope to feel sufficiently able to call 'united airlines' to change a flight

CALLING ALL ASTEROIDS PLEASE COME TO EARTH AT YOUR HIGHEST SPEED AT YOUR EARLIEST CONVENIENCE *CALLING ALL ASTEROIDS*

November

heard 'i feel like the hamburgers here probably aren't good' as 'i feel like i'm the happiest i've ever been' ~5am last night

ate a crepe in ~6 seconds in a ~$32 korean buffet

all i want to do is type 'i don't know what to do'

afraid to do anything public on internet except this tweet currently

argentina is shaped like a steak and famous for steaks

feel like it's been 2012 for ~10 years, unsure if i already tweeted this

feel like my eyeballs are trying to get away from me

rereading 'sent' emails to check for egregious errors

watching a video of myself eating a giant bowl of noodles in 2008

believed i was the devil last night in a manner that seems bleak

turned around in post office and saw an ominous, scared-looking, male midget wearing 'harry potter' glasses

feel like something is continually crying me into existence, like something is crying and i'm its tears and when it stops i'll disappear

feel like my most consistent sensation of being alive the past ~17 years is of low-level nausea from wanting to vomit my heart out of my body

me doing stand-up comedy: 'if an asteroid isn't coming to earth soon...why the hell are we here? [something re nasa]'

can't remember if 'fireman' is a thing

responded to email from 1 of my sarah lawrence students in less than 1 minute at 9:03 on a friday night

go shoplifting on black friday, relax/detox/fast in holding cells on saturday/sunday, return to reality on monday refreshed

December

i want to give a kind, tiny, docile, shy turtle a ~2-4 hour handjob

imagined a small, innocent, happy child crawling excitedly into something called a 'news tent' that functions like facebook's 'news feed'

i want to post everything online so i don't accidentally delete it

what if not enough people donate to wikipedia and it disappears

keep thinking 'if the world doesn't end dec 21 2012...'

imagined 1 of the pyramids from giza traveling pointy-end-first from somewhere inside the solar system toward my head

sperm whale are kind of shaped like xanax bars

kafka community college

a person's face is concentrated to their head's front half whereas a blue whale's face is spread throughout their body's front half

feel like my glasses (lens, frame) are egregiously blocking my vision

feel like decapitating myself to cure low-level nausea

under blanket with macbook with watery eyes dreading the future

didn't have enough cookies for every student to get 1 full cookie on last day of class because i ate most of 1 box of them on train there

kobo abe retitled his last/unfinished novel from 'flying man' to 'the spoon-bending boy' back to 'flying man' then back to 'the spoon-bending boy'*

imagined myself repeatedly 'turning around' to try to face myself to tell myself something and never succeeding, never learning what i knew

thought 'i'm going to be one of those people who live in the mountains alone, but i would never do that' while scrolling thru facebook

what if every culture and nostradamus had predicted the exact same date re 'end of world' but the date was like 50 trillion years away

macbook called 'macbook loneliness'

i want to be playing final fantasy 3 in 1991

2013

January

philip seymour hoffman as a professor with a giant blackboard in a lecture hall who uses a ladder to write 'fucked' in a ~20 minute scene

---

* According to an interview with his daughter at horagai.com/wwwithabe/xneri.htm.

if any comets/meteors/etc are reading this right now...i'm at 229 e 29 st

'ask me directions even though i'm wearing head-phones and walking away from you and there's 5-15 other people you could ask' tote-bag

thought 'no one understands me' in an indiscern-ible tone while looking at my instagram on com-puter screen and clicking things ~40% randomly

baked a frozen burrito at ~350 degrees for ~10 hours in oven

oprah's favorite bright eyes song is 'something vague'

gave directions to elderly asian in taipei airport by alternating saying 'i don't know' and 'seems to be that way' in semi-incoherent mandarin

people say 'embarrassed' instead of 'sorry' or 'ex-cuse me' in taiwan

keep visualizing lasagna 'undulating' in a manta-ray-like manner in taiwan 'the hunchback of notre dame' is called 'clock [word meaning "floor" in terms of "2nd floor" or "3rd floor"] weird person'

dreamed about baking rice crispy treats in an oven

memoir titled 'fucking insane'

can't think of a moment when it wouldn't be funny if i disappeared

thought 'lucifer' in reference to [what seemed to be 'nothing'] while pulling blanket over myself on bed

in a café responded to person saying my table is ready by drooling on my macbook and mumbling 'okay' in semi-incoherent mandarin

keep imagining myself 'strangling' my macbook

February

'dj unreliable sack of shit'

visible things are partially hidden because they have a surface to reflect light

the dalai lama has a constant fear of being fatally headbutted by a male caucasian with a huge beard

the dalai lama has recurring nightmares about being alone and helpless inside a submarine that's 'flying' out of the solar system

the dalai lama owes me $55,539.64

i lose followers whenever i tweet about the dalai lama

feel like i'm outsourcing the work of my life to my future self while doing the work that my past self has outsourced to my current self

realized somewhat ominously that a constant, the past ~10 years, in my life, is 'increasing # of increasingly complicated/longer passwords'

my dad said 'sticky cake' in mandarin quietly to himself and opened the refrigerator and closed it and walked away without getting anything

became aware of myself weakly thinking 'the impenetrable world of tao lin' in a mocking tone while cutting my hair

person averted their sight as i walked absently up a down escalator while maneuvering my iphone so the display wasn't sideways/upside-down

horror movie in which i discover both my parents have stayed up all night in separate rooms googling something like 'beige neckless giraffe'

my dad is watching 'ace ventura: pet detective' on tv

successfully convinced myself to indulge in short-term gratification by thinking 'there were millions of years between dinosaurs and humans'

eating 8 tiny containers of 'yo baby' yogurt

i want to say 'that was a dark period of my life' to oprah in reference to my entire life as a joke that she will seem to not 'get'

imagined myself impulsively saying 'anyone want to hear me yodel for 20 minutes?' to start a reading and doing it at the 1st indication of 'yes'

t-shirt that says 'i want to strangle an innocent stranger'

my bio: tao lin can speak 0 languages, he lives in manhattan

March

thinking thoughts like 'i need to use my brain to help me' that seem like thoughts i would not recommend for myself to think but i'm not sure

daydreamed about training 2 plants to manage my gmail

thought about writing a novel featuring 'time travel' and felt excited in a manner like no one has ever considered or done that before

imagined what a 'chicken monster' might look like and couldn't visualize anything other than a normal chicken moving insanely fast

movie in which dr frankenstein and his 'monster' prepare for a zombie invasion

what if i developed the incredible skill to easily make smoothies using only my hands (via scissoring motions and a form of juggling)

in 2032 jonathan franzen will become j26franzoid after successfully undergoing a controversial operation to 'computerize' 52% of his brain

sounded like the elevator said 'fucked' in a quiet-but-not-whispered voice as it landed on 1st floor and i laughed hysterically ~5 seconds

seated woman on c train lectured everyone, said 'we act like jesus is invisible when we go out to the clubs' and other things in a kind tone

April

was considering buying grapes from fruit-stand outside a deli when the sales person said 'hello' scaring me away

felt emotionally moved by woman saying 'sorry' to me after crossing the sidewalk in a manner causing me to stop a little unsure if there is or is not a common thing called 'face mat'

poetry collection titled 'alone in the hell of my existence'

thought 'my name is nicolai instafoam' and grinned alone in my room

feel like there was a nintendo game called 'hell fucked'

feel like 1 or 2 of the alien babies from 'alien' are in my chest

movie titled 'being john malkovich on 120mg adderall'

found a poem i wrote on paper with pencil in high school or college titled 'today's boredom is tomorrow's yesterday's boredom'

May

form of writing called 'extreme liveblogging' in which you type faster than you think and can read your subconscious monologue in real time maybe bought a 19.16lb watermelon for $13.22

'i officially hate myself in an earnest manner'
shirts/patches/stickers to distinguish from 'i hate
myself' shirts/patches/etc

editing my writing, at some point, has become
like trying to eat a salad on a plate made of shit
with utensils made of shit

gollum seems like the perfect pet to me...if i wanted a pet...i'd feel good nurturing and caring for
him and trying to make him happy

lost a plastic bag of oranges & frozen burritos
during the ~2 minute walk from gristedes to my
apartment building...backtracked and can't find...

if a blind person started strangling me for an unknown reason i feel like i'd probably think 'what
should i do' until i was dead

i haven't spoken yet today and i feel like i can
speak fluent spanish

conversation in which both people talk nonstop—
simultaneously hearing, considering, answering,
asking, planning, improvising

June

got an idea...lightweight/foldable structures that
attach to open refrigerators like tiny rooms which
you sit in to quickly cool yourself

idly imagined myself tearing out someone's
throat, i think, while thinking 'where are my
glasses' and looking for my iphone

rap song titled 'sausage cocaine hell'

dreamed i had time-traveled and was in my childhood home holding a block of ice and felt confused and woke

think i just now realized octopus have huge heads

feel like it's 2008 or 2009, definitely not anything
past 2011

imagine getting your head cut in half with a piece
of paper

imagined myself saying 'my brain is broken, my brain is broken' while holding my head and rapidly walking in circles around woody allen

on sunday everyone should spend 6 hours alone reading what they've published on the internet the past week

los angeles seems hellish to me

banana bread seems funny (tweeting this alone in a bar)

feel like every person including me is insane

in a dark room turn your iphone around and pretend you're looking at the internet as the screen shines light away from you

had a nightmare in which my band (me and 1 other person) broke into a bank at night to film a music video for a song called 'the fall'

i encourage people interested in terence mckenna, people interested in shamanism, depressed people, alienated people to come to my readings

looked at instagram on iphone (ostensibly looking for guggenheim directions) as 2 friends looked at their phones (ostensibly for same)

the year 19842012

July

imagined myself looking at twitter and old photos and other things on my iphone while unselfconsciously waiting in line to be incinerated

walking in search of coconut or almond yoghurt

i'm eating a salad in a movie theatre lobby instead of in my room for the air conditioning

if you believe you're in a maze you instantly gain purpose, but nothing matters until you fulfill that purpose, of exiting the maze

became aware of myself absently scrolling thru facebook thinking 'you're all fucked' while stoned and eating food with my other hand

think i might start talking to myself when alone

i want to buy an incredibly powerful sponge

feel like i could improvise olympics-level gymnastics in a life/death situation

imagined myself lying to everyone that i've read all of dostoyevsky

while trying to sleep felt that if people tried hard enough they could fly using only their bodies

does anyone else's entire life feel like déjà vu

August

manned mission into space with no return plan or destination

Looking at Twitter, Gmail, Instagram when people around me think I'm searching for info relevant to the conversation

Feel like I'm in an extremely low budget sci-fi movie that's millions of hours of footage that will never be edited into an actual movie

I'm in an internet café* in which a man seemed to have gained a free hour of internet usage by screaming 'fuck' repeatedly, it's 3:40am

I'm in an internet cafe in which I feel like all ~15 customers are friends because I think a man said 'who is that guy' re me, it's 3:57am

Cashier in grocery said '48.39' when my total was $19.54 and I gave her $20 and she gave me change and I left, we maintained neutral faces

Change your life by changing every aspect of your life

Living in low-level fear of becoming a serial killing cannibal

Feel like I can't remember the last time I looked at a non-full moon

Daydreamed about adopting a koala to live in my room with me

---

* By the Piccadilly Circus station in London.

Found a poem titled 'i want to email myself to an unknown email address' in my Gmail account from 2005

Dreamed the plot and most of the dialogue of a horror movie set in a suburban area with casinos

Earnestly thought 'I'll do something about it if it's still an issue after I die' about an aspect of my life and felt calmed

I'm increasingly convinced dying doesn't end consciousness

I think I can peel oranges extremely fast...like 'inhumanly' fast...

I can peel oranges faster than humanly possible... if you ever see me peeling one slowly or at a normal speed it's because I'm practicing

I can peel oranges at superhuman speed...

I'm losing followers...why...I'm sorry, I'm not actually sure how objectively fast I peel oranges...it just seemed really fast last night...

Experienced what tasted interestingly like a sugary sweetness in the stems of parsley

Architecture based on the structure of fruit

Anyone ever get the feeling your life is about to segue into a ~2-hour, understated, 'haunting, beautiful' horror movie?

I don't want to peel oranges anymore...too much pressure to be the fastest...too much pressure with little to zero benefits...

Might try to start talking extremely fast all the time

Sensed part of me trying to convince part of me I'm in a sci-fi movie and it's been my repressed, lifelong desire to live where I live

The first giant-octopus President of the United States

The next world-famous celebrity could be a krill, I really feel

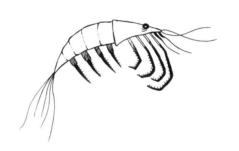

Talked at-length about my psilocybin experience involving 'alien possession'/[how to easily become messianic] to ~70 people today

Imagine getting sucked forward in time faster than you've ever experienced time and feeling a scary, mysterious, new dizziness

Unable to remember if I have a 'memory foam' mattress or not

I'm serious about the 'memory foam' mattress (didn't notice the potential joke until after tweeting it)

On 41st floor, looking at the city, intuited the blatant manner in which privacy seems to be a short-term, divisive, 'pessimistic' solution

September

Wanting greater degrees of 'freedom' (meaning wanting to exist in more dimensions) is as insatiable as wanting more [anything](?)

Sound of my refrigerator door closing seemed unexpectedly, eerily, very quiet

Supine on my bed planning where I'll buy a towel from

Began to assume the person bagging my groceries was doing it slightly slower than normal because she was multitasking 'cursing' me

Prepared to abandon ~95% of my life at almost any moment

Craving the slow, gradual fulfillment of a romantic desire

Sounds like the 3 plumbers in my bathroom are talking quietly so that I can't hear what they're saying

The plumbers have fucked up big-time, the superintendent is getting their phone # due to possible damages they've caused

Heard plumber say 'you got to be fucking shitting me'

I keep hearing the plumbers whispering, sounds like they're whispering...

Feel like I dreamed of a new way to sleep and slept that way last night after 'inventing' it in my dream

Feel like most of my life now is spent neurotically editing sentences

Felt like I didn't know what was going to happen when I couldn't decide which bananas to buy (they all looked almost the same)

I recommend blowdrying your face and other parts of your body

October

Waiting for the perfect moment to stop repeatedly refreshing 2-4 websites while sometimes clicking a link to some other website

Bought $15 ticket for buffet that opens at 6:30am, it's 5:56am

Feel like I'm constantly distracted from reality by premonitions of the most extreme, awkward thing that could happen or be said at any moment

At the hotel buffet my mom made a machine squirt milk incessantly and I told her to run away and she cowered a little toward me

UFO INVASION RED ALERT RED ALERT MAN THE BATTLE STATIONS IM SERIOUS NOW NOW GO EVERYONE NEEDS TO HELP NOW NO TIME TO EXPLAIN

Woody Allen movie in which he acts utterly out-of-control—screeching while insanely multitasking and verbally dominating everyone for 2 hours

Thought 'I'm getting better at golf' as a nonsequitur while peeing...

Rushing home to nap

Try to imagine something extremely difficult to imagine, like that would take years of work just to be certain it was imaginable

I'm in McDonald's using wifi and everyone that enters, in my peripheral vision, seems like they're coming in with a gun to rob this location

Feeling like every person in this McDonald's has

been at least peripherally involved in the making of at least 1 horrific snuff film

I'm in McDonald's reading the Wikipedia page for 'snuff film'

Felt sci-fi to get an email from a student in my class in 2012 at Sarah Lawrence

The low # of people wandering aimlessly inside the 24-hour Best Buy in Union Sq at 12:28am seems surreal, like there should be many more

My Halloween costume is my room (via 'wearing' my room during Halloween)

Have recently decided not to send 2 emails that would've, in 1st draft, begun with a variation of 'this seems insane, but'

Dreamed I was in a large social gathering on a variety of amphetamines talking idly to ~4 strangers at once with little interest but feeling ok

Thought of a way to name your company: [thing you're selling] [any animal] (Computer Frog, DVD Rhinosaurus)

Thought of a way to name your company: [any word] [any word] [thing you're selling] (Bag Tundra Computer, The At DVD)

Read 'Extra Cheesy Cheddar Bunnies Baked Snack Crackers' as 'Extra Cheesy Cheddar Bunnies Failed Snack Crackers'

Walked past woman seated alone in darkness in park and it looked like she was knitting but she was eating a giant piece of duck or chicken

What if it became 'cool' for kids in middle/high school to talk about 'peripheral vision', like if some band released a [abandoning tweet]

Made sustained and intense, I feel, eye contact with a small black dog across post office interior

A man rode by on street on a Segway with both hands in pockets wearing earphones staring straight ahead with unlit cigarette in mouth

November

Reminder to self: view life like it's an already-written book that I'm allowed to read once without stopping from beginning to end

Imagine if every pro basketball, baseball, football, hockey, soccer, tennis player, and boxer alive also each had their own monthly bookclub

Feeling unable to write an essay* about my inability to write the original essay I had committed to write

Got an idea...stand-up comedian that openly appears to be and actually is a robot (no skin or eyes, just metal-looking things and diodes)

Got an idea...pasta that, due to its specially designed shape, requires no straining (of water it's boiled in) to move from pot to wherever

What if every Smashing Pumpkins song ('Tonight, Tonight', '1979', 'Zero', 'Mayonnaise', etc) was about procrastination

Sitting in chair in my room typing this with right hand while sometimes sipping 'Kava stress relief' tea held in left hand and grinning

---

* Published in issue 127 of *Granta* and, on June 16, 2014, online at granta. com.

Performance art piece in which I create a real, concrete situation where I'm earnestly screaming 'I'm overdosing on stress relief' to people

On the way out of a cafe I think I unconsciously locked the door and couldn't get out until a middle-aged woman unlocked it for me I think

Dark comedy in which Werner Herzog can't stop lying and in every scene says 'I know it's going to seem like I'm lying, but' multiple times

Earnestly (almost in a tone of 'grave seriousness' maybe), very stoned, thought something like 'I need to stop joking around on Twitter'

December

Is anyone out there

Is anyone not out there

It looks like something like half my emails are from myself telling me to do certain things

Being John Malkovich Staring in Mock-Disbelief at a Peacock in a Zoo in a Misguided, Unsuccessful Attempt to Entertain Himself

Being John Malkovich for a Randomly Selected 90 Minute Segment of His Life

Being John Malkovich Forever

Being John Malkovich at His Absolute Worst in Both His Private Life and Onscreen Performances

Patiently Being John Malkovich

Memory of thinking I was going to need to say 'bleep bloop' much louder/clearer than feels normal for me if I wanted to be comprehensible

Alternate reality in which Obama is regularly photographed struggling to avoid being photographed eating cookies while in transit

Intuited exactly how to rearrange my room while looking at my room stoned

Systematically protecting oneself from depression and loneliness

Thought 'who's going to be my next victim' in a distracted, comatose manner while scrolling through Gmail to choose an email to respond to

Living in fear of one's own antisocial tendencies

2014

January

Having a premonition that 2014 will be ~60% dreary/neutral, ~25% blunt in a painful way maybe, ~15% colorful in a pastel/spotted manner

Sensing flying fish articles on the internet will increase in 2014 just a little

Felt endeared/amused by my internal monologue saying 'put away the 2nd piece of carrot cake now' in a half-joking maybe but also stern tone

Sensing 2018 will be when things happen

Performance art piece in which for 1 year I don't use email and set my Gmail to auto-respond

'Sounds great, thank you' to every email

The distracting feeling of disbelief when I'm finally doing something I've procrastinated on for a notable amount of time

Fantasized about adopting a toy poodle last night while trying to sleep

Imagine being one of the humans who was born in 34,563BC and died in 34,533BC

Low self-esteem caused by reoccurring nightmares featuring helplessness, incompetency, confusion, and an overall lack of efficacy

3:40am seems like both a lunar and solar time, with an ability to especially 'cool' or 'warm' one in a pleasurable manner maybe

Performance art piece in which I lure the CIA into assassinating me in a manner that can't be proven or disprove

Mist from the shower in my hotel room set off the fire alarm

February

Rating things by how likely you are to forget the thing in whatever situation

Felt able to control my experience of the water's temperature to a degree that I unconsciously smiled while showering very stoned

Targeted pheromone transmission as timed telepathy

A country of millions of people trained to remotely fly micrograms of LSD/[anything] into people's systems as their full-time job

JFK international dystopian airport

Changing interests to gain perspective on your interests

2 people repeatedly alternating convincing the other they're conscious in ever more elaborate and surprising ways

My refrigerator is so loud it woke me multiple times last night

The dim, constant, vaguely confusing, lifelong/ unaddressed intuition that all pleasure, even mentally derived pleasure, is 'the' distraction

Feeling the sun thru the earth at night

Hallucinated a tiny bird floating up briefly into view outside my 4th floor window to monitor my activities for the CIA

Intuited a feeling of intimacy and friendship in the relationship between the human species and the orange fruit while eating one

I feel that I can for the first time understand how people earnestly have worshipped and do worship oranges (or any fruit, vegetable, plant, etc)

The relationship between humans and oranges goes back ~7 million years or more, the relation- ship between individuals lasts years/decades

Sensed something like the color orange 'winking blankly' at me from a science-fictional distance/ vacuum-thing re my orange fruit tweets

Imagined myself tickling my parents for the 1st time that I can currently remember ~4 weeks ago, was surprised

Science-fiction movie in which extraterrestrials do something absurd/baffling to Earth and the motive is that it's art, to them, they feel

Discerning a pattern and doing the same thing again anyway (this time watching it happen, so privately having a different experience of it)

Artist whose manifesto is 'if I kill myself, your investment instantly appreciates; if I live, I offer an option to sell back at 200% in 5 years'

Artist whose manifesto is simply, misanthropically/preemptively 'I don't want to argue with you'

Felt selfconscious on plane (middle seat) drawing a maze while watching a movie in which, it was revealed, an insane murder-suspect drew mazes

Creating the opposite of community

Sitting on my pilates mat sharpening my colored pencils

Try getting very stoned and staring into a bright lightbulb

March

A pigeon landed on a branch outside my 4th floor window (not too close, kind of sneakily/subtlety) to spy on me briefly and flew away suddenly

Getting stoned and listening to music and crying

Reading some incoherent-seeming emails, sending some incoherent-seeming emails

Remembered a boy who was so popular in ~4th grade that he'd idly say who he wanted to sit by in assemblies and his people would arrange it

Twitter accounts that you can't distinguish if they're publicly sent messages to 1 person or public messages

Intuited the evolutionary basis for procrastination being that it allows time for your unconscious to work on whatever problem/task

Observed a pigeon sprint across a sidewalk toward a piece of bread other pigeons were swarming around and eating earlier today

Created an extremely pessimistic-looking mandala

When you want to be destroyed by an asteroid/apocalypse it never happens, like ever, for anyone probably, or extremely rarely maybe

Imagined I was a pleased/complacent but alert flounder on a seafloor while lying on my side on my bed

Realized I've rarely said 'I feel' in Mandarin

I say/think 'I feel' constantly in English

Poetry collection titled 'officially waiting for Indian food'

Imagined myself decorating an apartment with tiny pieces of broccoli and cauliflower

Novel titled I Recommend My Previous Novels

Feels like I'm seeking permanent transcendence as a possible outcome for any activity

Deliberately halfhearted/halfassed novel titled It Is What It Is that costs half the price of other novels

April

Bouncy ball that doubles as a print book somehow, bouncy ball-book hybrid

If something in your life seems 'wrong' maybe it's because a # of your unread emails have been permanently deleted without your knowledge

Sci-fi movie in which people spend most of their recreational time building shrines/temples dedicated to other people in their lives

All my hundreds(?) of premonitions of the end of the world, or at least the end of the world for myself, have been wrong so far

Discovered I can use watermelon/grapefruit water (via peels or the fruit itself) to clean hard surfaces like my floor and desk

Lying in bed like a giant lobster

Lying in bed like a cold burrito

May

Being emotional alone in my room

Cleaning my floor with watermelon

Woody Allen sci-fi movie about a species that requires 6 individuals to have sex and reproduce

Read 'Strawberry Jelly Roll' as 'Singularity Jelly
Roll'

Felt amused/entertained/distracted by a de-
pressed-looking, poodle-like dog passing in other
direction on sidewalk

Person peacefully 'nodding out' in statue-like,
half-diagonally bent stance swaying curbside at
busy intersection in light rain by Union Square

My parents said when I was 1 and saw the horses
in Central Park I laughed nonstop for 10 minutes

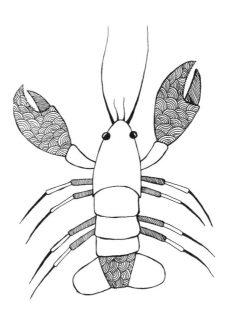

The more I think about it, the same uncertainty I feel

Zany/slapstick sci-fi movie in which only babies <15 months can time travel

Imagined myself buying a toy poodle and talking to it nonstop

June

Imagining oneself meditating as a method for meditating

I have enough dulse in my room for maybe ~20000 salads

Hallucinated Tupac, or a voice that sounded like Tupac, commenting on my drawing in a nice, encouraging, insightful way as I was drawing it

July

Found on my Gmail tasks list: 'Tao Lin is in simulation not us'

High-seeming # of very elderly people in computer lab today

Novel titled Self Publish Next Novel and Don't Do Interviews/Press

Looked outside window at 6 lights in the distance and my first thought was something like '6, that allows me to procrastinate 6 more minutes'

The feeling of being commanded by my internal monologue to do things as I partly narrate to myself what to do and continuously comply

Strawberries with guacamole

August

Developing a refrigerator phobia I think

'Keeping it "real"' alone in my room

September

Performance art where every email reply I ever send has to be the exact # of words of the email it's replying to otherwise I 'can't' respond   .

Alternating bites of banana and nibbles of jalapeño

November

Splurged on colored pencils

2011

May

what would a frozen onion be like...

June

my eyeballs

butterballs

the law offices of turkey, iphone, and buttermilk

my eyeballs...

mexican deli workers seem unpretentious

July

there's so many different kinds of apes and monkeys...i think...

i feel no desire to eat pretzels

'thousand island dressing' seems troubling

emitted 'mmoohuphm'

thought 'my head' holding my head

typed 'balooga with g'

memory of being lost in megan's gmail account
while on my computer

thought 'juejue'

thought 'mucho gusto' while scrolling up/down
gmail, i don't know what it means

thought 'should i cook a dead fish' and felt attracted to eating the skin on the side of a normal fish
that has been grilled

seems...easy to fly...to simply levitate my body
into the air

earnestly feel motivated to 'keep it real' more after looking at a lot of rapper things on wikipedia/ youtube

August

spain seems arid

80 degrees seems arid

typed answers to email-interview questions at what felt like 'record speed' while sitting on toilet

typed previous tweet at what felt like 'record speed'

thought 'is planking* sexy...can it be sexy...'

distantly considered having a different twitter account for every tweet i ever tweet

unconsciously typed 'fish' into twitter after hearing someone say 'fish'

---

* Thing people were doing where you lie facedown with a stiff body on [anything] and photograph and put it online.

nodded at @meganboyle at the same time she nodded at me after we both glanced at popcorn

which fast-food place has waffle fries...thought it was wendy's but i see people with normal fries here...

wendy's has added packets of 'pure sugar' now to their condiment selections, i see

someone should have a nightmare where they're forced to locate an airport's 'ass'

if my plane is crashing i'll spend my final moments editing my final tweet

feel like it would be something like 'spending final moments alive editing an earlier draft of the tweet you're reading'

eating a raw 'prune turnover' ~70% for the purpose of helping me sleep

mooched 'prozac nation' via bookmooch.com

watching 'world of warcraft' addiction things on youtube while exercising

feels like i'm 'seething' with the inability to sleep...

felt briefly '100% certain' i'll never finish my third novel

'lightly' studied the thought 'too old to die at 27' for profundity

i keep thinking 'computer' or 'computer screen' while trying to do things on the internet

discerned what i'm doing right now as 'livetweeting my nothing'

thought 'i'm nothing, i'm doing nothing' while clicking twitter things

feel like 'sending out an alert' that juicing frozen kale produces no juice, feel like doing this via @ tao_linalerts*

---

* Doesn't exist.

read 'poetry' on my 'tumblr feed' as 'poeetry or 'pooetry' and felt interested in looking at the word more then saw it was 'poetry'

hamish should be a new kind of hummus #thefuturelivetweet*

whenever it shows a new room i imagine myself lying on the floor #thefuturelivetweet

i made lasagna manually in college 5-10 times

thought about initiating some kind of contest between @tao_linunedited and @tao_lin in which i'd be able to be a 3rd thing

September

unexpectedly feeling a desire to watch the movie bowfinger

the idea of a 'world war' seems insane...

thought 'honeygringle mcschnoodleginkens'

---

* *The Future* (2011) is a movie by Miranda July starring herself and Hamish Linklater.

thought 'binky mc' ('mc' like the 'mc' in 'mcdon-ald's') and stopped thinking suddenly

briefly considered inviting like 10 people to come to my room right now to help me write my novel

'find myself' yearning 'once again' for a device that makes you sleep immediately...that one can wear on one's head or something...*

feel like many more people should be tweeting about their eyeballs, that eyeballs should be of strong/immediate interest to more people

thought 'internet tweeting spree'

sneezing uninhibitedly feels like a unique kind of 'screaming' where one doesn't need to exert any energy

imagined someone in 2089 typing in 'tao lin quotes' in google and reading my previous tweet

---

* I wrote about this in a dystopian short story for BBC Radio 4 called 'A Message of Unknown Purpose' which aired June 22, 2014.

lost 2 papaya halves in my room...unable to find the 2 papaya halves i brought into my room to eat...

officially 'giving up' the search for the 2 papaya halves i brought into my room to eat...

dreamed i bought 'diablo 3' from a walgreens-type store while looking at notebooks/folders for 'novel-writing organization' purposes

'peaking' on 1x 'st. john wort's' tea-bag, 1x 'green tea' tea-bag, 1x 'chai [something]' tea-bag

vaguely sensed the concrete existence of various foods in stores and restaurants in a certain radius of my room while in my room

having 'weakly disturbing' images of waffles with pasta on top

keep picturing waffles and, on a separate plate or directly on top, pasta...

repeatedly refreshing websites in an 'insane' manner

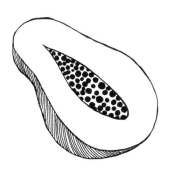

October

thesaurus.com's definition of 'phase' is 'period in life of something'

committed to watching a 6-part jfk conspiracy theory thing on youtube

went into public with an 'armor' of earplugs, sunglasses, large headphones, xanax today

experiencing problems spelling 'able to be disassembled' as one word

i recommend wearing earplugs when showering

supine in darkness feeling aversion toward my blogs' urls

November

opened a gabriel garcia marquez biography and read 'He was pumped up, high on literary narcotics.'

thought 'i don't want my internet presence to be this big, to have so many parts to it' with an earnest sensation of helplessness worried about what to do about the 'problem' of having 2 twitter accounts

anne sexton's sister's husband's name was 'brad jealous'

feeling more worried than any previous time, i think, about how to resolve my 'problem' of having 2 twitter accounts

feel like now is the time for a meteor to strike me fatally or someone to randomly murder me

December

manually creating 'egg drop soup'

novel titled 'drug metabolizer' about a man who claims he's metabolizing as many drugs as possible to 'destroy' them

feel like i don't remember 2011

had a nightmare i was in jail but easily adapted by making a tamale joke when another inmate tried to make me his 'bitch' i think examining my nightmare, it seems i was already in jail when 2 men came to arrest me, then i was brought like 2 rooms away, i think

seems 'extremely weird' to me that it's 6:30pm right now

2012

February

i can easily imagine it already being 2018, which makes me feel like the next 6 years will have no effect on me

lately when i walk by someone and they move their phone to their head...i think they're calling someone to come kill me

thought of my bed as my 'house'

remembered i have ~3000 words of 'shoplifting shoplifting from american apparel from urban outfitters' but can't find it anywhere*

---

* I found this and it begins: "Should I really write *Shoplifting Shoplifting from American Apparel from Urban Outfitters*," said Sam returning with Michelle to his apartment after buying pasta from a deli to eat during *The Royal Tenenbaums*, which they'd wanted to rewatch after rewatching

email from mom: '...the drawing contest is interesting. The cat won is soooo obese.'*

eating lasagna in a taxi cab

email from mom: 'Muumuu house is such a good name...'

March

uptown astor place 6 train isn't in service

account called @tao_linhelpful** for helpful tweets

June

bought ~$46 ebook***

Rushmore at Sunshine Cinema on methadone a few nights ago and both liking it more now than in any of their respective previous viewings, when (this was unsaid, but Sam felt they were both aware of its relevance) they hadn't been on drugs.

* I had a cat-drawing contest on my Tumblr. I forgot about this until re-reading this tweet for this book. I deleted my Tumblr in August 2013.

** Doesn't exist.

*** *The Philosophy of Schopenhauer* (1983) by Bryan Magee.

August

i recommend blending watermelon and any greens, it tastes like just watermelon

September

listening to terence mckenna* and the things he seems energized by are expressed in my novel as sources of bleakness and confusion

2013

February

i calculated it, and i think the size of a 3-yr-old child compared to the earth is like 1 minute in a 25-year-old's life, does this make sense

---

* For more on McKenna read my 12-part column Tao of Terence at vice. com.

2011

June

Not better. Not worse. Not the same. Just different.

2012

February

Had been avoiding "The Last Days of Disco" because I thought it was something set in Mexico filmed in the 50s or 60s.

August

Person who owes me 3 klonopin texted that they owe me 1 but will give me 2. I texted "U owe me 3."

I need to develop a fan base separate from the other Tao.

I think a variation of "no more fucking around" an average of ~5x/day. Average is skewed heavily by days I think it ~100x.

Sent/received ~25 texts, ~25 of the shittiest texts ever sent/received, whose sole purpose is to get 3 klonopin I'm owed, to no avail.

Sent ~10 unanswered texts to person who owes me 3 klonopin over ~50 hours until they responded they owe me 2 and "chill out."

September

Googled "air through window" to find out how to describe air going into a room through a window.

Imagined myself pushing a button that says "procure" to receive xanax.

2 employees at this ice cream store look like the singer from Anti-Flag.

I'm being exaggeratedly charismatic at LensCrafters on xanax. Feel like a jackass, grinning like a shithead.

Locked out of my room at a critical weekend of my life.

Lying in taxi with conventionally horrible posture.

My main website seems horrible.

I feel uncomfortable looking at ~95% people on the street...uncomfortable and insane.

Got 2/3 klonopin I'm owed after ~60-100 texts spanning ~20 days.

Stole 2 grapes from Dean and Delucca.

Thought "I want to be on 2mg xanax" while crawling across my floor to get something from my desk.

I keep hearing "Fur Elise" on repeat, only the 1st part, in a non-annoying/non-enjoyable manner, like to the left of me, faraway but close.

I think my building's super is framing me. Feel like this is the kind of thing a person like me should commit suicide to get out of.

Imagined people looking around my room and using my yoga mat to wrap my corpse.

Feels like 1998 right now outside.

Feel like I'm going to see an acquaintance walking around drunk outside in next hour.

I "have to" use tiny font when editing novel because I can't look at it if it seems too big because it's so bad.

I can't believe it's 2012, feel like it's 2003 or 2006. Also feel like its been 2012 for like 5 years.

I've trained myself to not believe I like anything I write if I haven't edited it like 20 times. Doesn't seem good maybe.

October

Accidentally texted drug dealer a text including "...maybe we should kill ourselves tonight" in it and he ignored it.

Ingested xanax to enhance the flavor of Newman-O's and ate all of them before xanax had taken effect.

Thought "I can feel the xanax coming out of my eyeballs" in reference to just normally being on xanax.

Eating ice cream and molly and probably a little xanax for breakfast at ~4PM.

Thought "if I die before my book comes out…" in an earnestly curious tone. Then "that seems good" in a normal, colloquial tone.

Analyzing why feeling euphoria makes me want to die while peaking on molly carrying a huge sack of books.

Thought "my introspective molly trip" while walking thru deli carrying coconut waters peaking on molly.

I like in DFW bio[*] where he's quoted calling something a "fucking, fucking nightmare" with "fucking" in italics both times.

Supine on sidewalk tweeting this tweet.

---

[*] *Every Love Story Is a Ghost Story: A Life of David Foster Wallace* (2013).

Thought "yawning xanax" while walking across room yawning to get to bathroom to pee.

Creating a cucumber-spinach-orange smoothie using a Monster-brand "absolutely zero" energy drink as the liquid base.

Smoothie in [previous tweet] tasted distinctly like the movie FernGully, which I haven't thought of in ~10 years and don't think I've seen.

Got ideas for ~4-8 books while showering on ~25mg adderall.

It's taking ~15 texts, ~5 phone calls, and ~10 emails to fail to confirm a time/place to eat dinner with my family.

Felt emotionally unstable during Looper[*].

Stopped myself from crying (or, in a kind of confused emotional state, laughing, I think) probably ~12x during Looper.

---

[*] *Looper* (2012) is "a science fiction action thriller" (Wikipedia) starring Bruce Willis.

Marie Calloway just said "talk to you later" in what I discerned as an unintentionally cold tone while entering @nytyrant party at KGB bar.

If I get arrested tonight I'll be going to jail with DMT, xanax, "roxy" crumbs, adderall, draft of essay for n+1-affiliated anthology*.

Read 090ZX as xanax.

~$200 shopping-spree at FedEx-Kinkos on 30mg adderall. In cab back to apartment now.

November

Accidentally incinerated ~$72 worth of adderall (via garbage chute) due to inattentiveness that was probably partially caused by xanax.

2013

April

Anyone know exactly how benzos are an improvement on barbiturates? Feel like...they must actually be different...not better/worse.

---

* MFA vs NYC: The Two Cultures of American Fiction (2014).

Elaborate plan to manually time-release my xanax via complex sets of skillfully improvised, mentally draining algorithms.

May

Became aware of my internal monologue "threatening" ("...better work this time...") the xanax/adderall in me at length.

Feeling idly, emotionlessly suicidal.

June

Missed ~6PM flight by sleeping ~2PM to ~10PM.

Retreating from @tao_lin to here.

Went to sleep after retreating from @tao_lin to here.

African-American man named "Neo-Ryan" (?) holding cigarette said hi to me on street, said he was friends with David Fishkind's girlfriend.

Shouted "can't you just put vodka in cheese?" at @miragonz and @samcke while stoned and unconsciously unwrapping a pot brownie.

Heard @miragonz say "...when I was adopted..." I think.

July

Mira Gonzalez (@miragonz) multiplied 3.5 by 6 in a situation without time constraints or any other stress factors. Her answer was 15.

Excitedly "grabbed" 2 cans of zero-calorie Cherry Coke in deli while stoned.

Laughed alone in my room, on and off, for maybe 30 seconds, imagining myself blurbing every book "The new Catcher in The Rye."

Thought "I always knew I'd be more popular than @tao_lin8/@tao_lin3" from perspective of @tao_lin33 in a lying-during-awards-speech tone.

Thought "The Remains of the Day" (Ishiguro novel I haven't read) as a nonsequitur while pouring remaining crumbs of xanax in my mouth.

2014

January

Love at first sight / stereotype at first sight.

April

Crying 2:59AM

2012

November

Rambled in email to Sarah Lawrence class then began paragraph with 'basically'

When most of your thoughts are censored to a third tier twitter account

Teaching John Barth and Donald Barthelme on large dose of xanax today

Creating color-coded charts for my Sarah Lawrence students if there's enough time

I'll probably rant about gender and race to Sarah Lawrence class today

Post brain damage output

Yawning alone on metro north train on molly depressed an hour from NYC

I only know 1 person who follows this account, I see

Struggling to get new email account to get new twitter account

Worked on ~600-word thing for $300 for ~20 hours over ~2 months. Refunded $300 and flaked.

Pooping alone in candle lit bathroom, my bathroom

Putting xanax powder on your crotch to get oral sex

Today's gonna be ok due to drugs 'whew!'

my last contact lenses shriveled up and I have no glasses

I can't see what I'm typing unless I stop walking and move the screen closer to my face

I should teach class blindfolded

I want to spend 30 minutes of class time trying to sell stolen sunglasses to my students for my future biographer

I'm officially beginning my next novel today I think, gonna be a meta thing focusing on addressing my future biographer[*]

Investigative journalism on my own life as it happens

Part of me keeps thinking 'I earnestly think there is something wrong with me' but then other parts think other things

If I teach again I'm renaming my class 'bleak literature'[**]

can foresee when adderall without xanax will seem hellish

---

[*] Haven't considered this idea for more than ~5 minutes total I think since this tweet.

[**] I'm teaching again in Sarah Lawrence's MFA program in Spring 2015 and the class is still called The Contemporary Short Story.

Moving toward thing where 2 or more drugs are needed to feel not suicidal

Person I think I'm kind of officially maybe dating stole 2 adderall from me

unconsciously flushed 5 30mg adderall wrapped in paper towel down toilet, realized ~20 minutes later

Making cantaloupe cucumber smoothie with liquid base of flat ginger kombucha

My unrar thing completely disappeared

drifting further n further away from happiness... as seen from a distance...on a movie screen...by a happier, less 'dead' version of myself

My future biographer would want me to openly snort cocaine off my hand while teaching class, reviewers of my future biography also would want

Depends on who my future biographer is, they'll all want different behavior

Me vs my future biographers

I bought all my Sarah Lawrence students, even the 3 auditors, copies of NOON*

I'm the proud owner of over 1000mg addy

Soon my Sarah Lawrence class will be over, 4 days after that the world is supposed to end

Another Sarah Lawrence student followed me on main twitter

There's a pile of Internal Revenue Service papers in corner of my room accumulating interest/penalties since July

Without 1-3 friends who don't feel negatively re me i would feel insane and earnestly seek help like in church maybe...maybe

2013

June

I encourage people to review my books on Amazon while peaking on MDMA or Adderall

---

* Annual literary magazine founded in 2000 by Diane Williams.

July

I've gotten comfortable using ~8 Twitter accounts. It's become natural to me. Like I need this many. To feel ok. To express myself.

Haven't used benzos/amphetamines in ~7 (?) days

Looks like I'm not gonna succumb to adderall/benzos, kind of surprised

August

I deleted multiple accounts and threw away my MacBook while 'possessed' by an alien entity after eating 3-4 (?) grams psilocybin

Going to library to discern my Internet situation... feel overwhelmed by the task...wish it would all just disappear...I think...

I'm grinning...

Became aware that I was attentively watching an imaginary basketball game while trying to sleep with eyes closed

Nibbling Ben Brooks' bitcoin xanax

Eating a giant pile of rice

Lost a baggie of weed while stoned, seeking weed in the UK, no social interaction

Having premonitions that Australia will be hellish

Calling all serial killers: I'm at Heathrow airport terminal 3 international departures with negative money and no ticket

The ingenious 'bloodstream technique' of drug smuggling

Might hang out in Heathrow ~20hrs

Thought of a way the Internet has done something, it's harder to remember who did or said what

Woke ~7:30am, ate oranges, showered, ate an avocado and I'm ready to sleep now, 8:39am

Getting stoned off red wine-macadamia oil-weed sauce after completing a piece on my childhood toy poodles[*]

September

Malaysia Airlines commercial seemed incredibly manipulative/misleading #stokerlivetweet[**]

Trailer for movie about Princess Diana seems incredibly...the same...misleading... #stokerlivetweet

If anyone ever sees me anywhere (but especially outside NYC) feel free to offer me marijuana, via email or in person

I...people keep shittalking things to me expecting me to agree or something, but I feel aversion to it

Feeling egregious I think

---

[*] Published in issue 88 of *The Fader* and, on October 11, 2014, online at fader.com.

[**] *Stoker* (2013) is a movie directed by Park Chan-wook.

Craving ravioli

I'm more interested in Buddhist/Schopenhauer-like philosophies while stoned

Craving twizzlers, ravioli, soup

Ex gf's ex bf arrested for heroin possession

Panhandler said I look like Jackie Chan and, very stoned, I laughed genuinely 5-10 seconds

Feel like the last 4 hours of my life, doing mundane things alone in my room, have been 'hilarious'

Repeatedly thought 'life of pi beef stroganoff' in reference to nothing while trying to sleep

Found ~.7mg xanax on the carpet in a hotel room in Amsterdam...

Realized the xanax I found on carpet is mine...has been in my pocket for like 15 days, thru ~7 airports, I think...

October

Using adderall high to return to room to get/use adderall to return to library (remember this day next time I'm trying to resist adderall)

Felt relief while tentatively committing to 2 years of no friends/girlfriend

While trying to decide something my mind became, it seemed, blank, then the decision seemed already in action

Who tweeted that tweet about it being possible that hot dogs are the sole cause of depression, anyone have link

Became aware of trying to pretend to myself that I was asleep last night while stoned with eyes closed trying to sleep

I keep remembering, only after already leaving apartment without spraypaint, to spraypaint a hamster in the style of Banksy

Have cried from [not pain/sadness] for extended periods of time while very stoned and on a little mushrooms 2-3x in past week

'Good morning, this is Dan Rather, with the news. Today, [person] died in an insanely nonhumorous manner'

November

Sentence from email from French journalist: 'I received Taipei last week, I almost finished it and I loved it.'

Had extreme-seeming dream in which I kept becoming irreversibly formless to travel thru the world to escape an indiscriminating force

Thought 'if this turns bad I'm fucked' with some earnestness while laughing uncontrollably to incapacitation at something vague while very stoned

Leisurely smoking via new vaporizer while listening to Five String Serenade by Mazzy Star via iPhone speaker tweeting this with 1 hand

December

Felt myself feeling fascinated by an elderly woman looking thru glass into a refrigerated storage area of hummus and other things in grocery store

Worked on an essay for pretty much like 20 hours nonstop

Repeatedly read 'trapeze' as 'vyvanse' while stoned. Like while staring at the word.

Schopenhauer would've been fascinated by psychedelics I feel

If you ask me for directions in person while I'm stoned I'm very helpful/caring

2014

January

The Art of Blacking Out on Stimulants

Feeling at ease inside Curry in a Hurry*

Reoccurring nightmares of being alone and helpless in difficult, complicated situations

currently drinking 2 kinds of soda, eating dates,

---

* Indian restaurant in Manhattan at 119 Lexington Ave.

smoking weed, listening to julia holter, reading 'food of the gods', sending emails

Death releasing you into a lower dimension

At a social thing stoned asked 'what the hell is everyone talking about' as a nonsequitur to 2 people as ~15 people talked seemingly nonstop

February

Urge to leave society upon losing cards/keys

Noticed my left arm looks healthier than normal

Both arms look healthier than normal

grabbing the arm of my chair in an extremely tight grip and pretending it's stuck, my hand is stuck to the chair, while very stoned currently

On good terms again with my building's superintendent and his wife finally, I feel, after ~2 years

My lifestyle is so far away from a tribal lifestyle... so far away

Almost eerily far away

Living the eerie, solitary lifestyle of the octopus

Derived almost sexual pleasure from mostly unconsciously conducting Chopin piano with legs/
feet while supine on my bed

Less able to ignore and more able to detect the
subconscious motives of my behavior while
stoned

March

Have a vague crush on Filipino (?) health food
store cashier

Keep hearing Spanish/Catalonian people say what
sounds like 'mucho pasta' (this was ~6 weeks ago)

Realized I've spent like...a nonhumorously shocking amount of time neurotically editing and wor-
rying about paragraph breaks in my writing

I think I haven't not felt afraid to some degree
to sit or stand alone (not lay) in a nearly but not
pitch black room in ~5 years

Feel comfortably/pleasurably like I'm wearing a layer of air currently

Having the lingering suspicion I've committed many faux pas in my past 2-5 social situations

April

Subtly, very slightly, I feel, slowly, and briefly 'invaded' an elderly woman's private space in post office line while very stoned

Thought 'an entire loaf of bread is fortuitous' as a nonsequitur while feeling nauseated for emotional reasons

Post office employee held book of stamps at me and I went to get with 2 fingers but closed my fingers on air ~4 inches from stamps

Felt an urge to go back and relive ~1998-2006, the most obscure lonely private period of my life

I recommend blending cucumber and coconut water

A classic short story that uses the umbrella as a metaphor for life but in an extremely complicated, 'insane' way

May

Too depressed to repeatedly refresh 3-4 sites while occasionally some other site

Releasing only art one feels 'ashamed' of as a kind of self-help something

The way a psychedelic seems to want me to rationalize my behavior into being caused by it seems like it's an intelligence promoting itself

Hallucinated a high pitched owl-sounding, tiny puppy bark-like sound that echoed rapidly and made me smile

5 minutes in silent darkness

June

I think I've felt that benzos make colorful lights more vibrant mostly because lights were dulled while not on benzos maybe

I've been raw vegan and sober except weed ~7 days

Feel like flaking on an article I committed to by leaving society

Email from mom said 'almost half of Africa is owned by China'

Remembered the band No Means No

My @tao_lin3 identity

August

Half consciously killed and smoked a mosquito

Supine on yoga mat smoking weed

November

Extremely worried about my websites

Thought 'I don't matter' as a nonsequitur while rinsing & putting away a fork

Viewed my gmail as a radioactive 'dead zone'

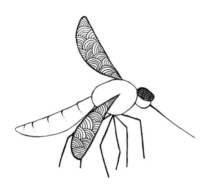

@tao_lin8*

2012

November

Lorrie Moore published 3 depressed/suicid-al-woman stories in a row when ~32 I think: 'You're Ugly, Too', 'Willing', 'The Jewish Hunter'

If I get rich and undepressed I'll make a nonprofit organization to fact-check published articles and teach people never to trust to the media

anyone awake

i'm not @tao_lin4

huddled inside my shirt on xanax listening to 8-bit music I chose by clicking randomly in iTunes feel-ing cold

December

Thought 'manually ate a cheese salad' while trying to past tense narrate that I had eaten cheese and, separately, lettuce

I'm behaving under the assumption that the world will end Dec 21 and also the saying 'it's the journey that counts not the goal' I think

I need someone to force me into some other kind of life never mind

Is there free rehab? The rehab industry seems egregiously lecherous, profiteering

I inevitably think of every week as 'hell week' in a manner like it's a rarity

I've recently stolen probably >$250 of incense and incense holders and other incense things from Whole Foods

Thought 'is prison free?' with some confusion

'bacon egg ham and cheese sandwich' has pork twice and pork is a different word for bacon or ham

i should divide my net worth in my will to followers of this account 90%, followers of @tao_lin3 5%, @tao_lin2 4%, @tao_lin 1%

feel impressed i did the math right, or that it seems right

Cheerful Mexican delivered me chicken and ice cream shake

Mira Gonzalez is the Hispanic girl in Odd Future

I've been ingesting xanax and carbs steadily for like 5 hours in an effort to get sleepy and sleep but I feel more energy gradually

Feel insanely, almost completely nonhumorously depressed I think

stared down at hands on keyboard thinking 'i should have used xanax not adderall and concerta...'

Had a thought I feel uncomfortable tweeting here

should i buy something like 200 xanax

Asked drug dealer for all the xanax he can get

Drug dealer outsourced to his uncle 'Tito' who is
47

Haiku / joy leaves me alone / as I walk to ATM /
nothing more to add

Tito who looks 35 said he's 55 and was sent in
1973 to the North Pole in the army for communi-
cations then Saigon

Pretty sure Tito sold me 5 bars I was supposed to
get free but I let him

Is Tito 55 or 47 and why would my dealer, who
said he's in Portland, lie about that?

I think Tito said on phone he's 4"10' but in person
was maybe 5'8"

I think Tito kept 3 bars for himself

Wonder if Tito started talking about his time in
'the service' to let me know he could probably easily kill me with his hands

Nothing makes sense in this brief drug encounter

Tito referenced 'the North Pole' as 'down there' ('they sent me down there')

I told him he looks 35

escaping drugs via taiwan

my parents will save me 'after all'

Should I attempt an 180mg addy binge

anyone there

Noticed I've begun at some point in past 5-15 hours to think 'please die today' to myself instead of the usual 'someone please kill me'

Library closed next 3 days nothing to do

@tao_lin33*

---

* This account's profile picture was a Photoshop drawing of Harry Potter by me.

2012

December

Used 90mg addy, hate my life

singer of the band 'I hate myself' is probably still alive, and will probably outlive me, as will most singers of emo bands I like probably

Been up 34hrs, 240mg addy, 52mg concerta, ~3.5 xanax. Do not want to sleep, sleep = travel to new shitty day while this day is already here

Napped ~70min. Getting earnest seeming texts from Joseph that he really, like more than normal, I feel, wants to die tonight.

Lying on side on bed unable to sleep dreading future

Didn't sleep except ~70 minute thing I think and don't feel sleepy, will I please PLEASE die today

I believe I could use as much meth as those people in ads and look like a model in terms of skin and if i really wanted like also muscles/hair

If you leisurely use 1/4 xanax bars, and have like 50, and just keep using 1/4, it can rapidly seem to get 'out of hand' big time

I don't remember what caused me to want to make this account, what person I suspected [never mind remembered]

I'm going to a Wall Street Journal house party

Bringing heroin xanax percocet addy to WSJ house party

I have no desires currently in a non-buddhist manner

slept via percocet, back at same computer typing this now, worried about today

Unsure if another twitter is needed for current thoughts

Hiding under blanket thinking about my own depression 830am

reread tweets from this account and thought 'no wonder I feel like shit now, damn'

feel better knowing i 'should' feel horrible re past ~8 days that I see on this twitter, feel more confident and willing to use more drugs now

When I read any tweet where anyone is using drugs I feel safer and usually also encouraged to use more drugs

I should call every time I use drugs a relapse

thinking of the next 3 days as 'hell week'

Really feels like my heart is crying

Feel like I've gone thru 3-6 'hell week's in past ~5 days

Bringing wine to class, last day of class

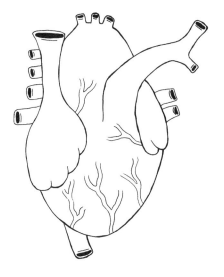

Bringing enough cookies for 1 cookie per student

Bringing not enough cups

Keep imagining myself beginning class 'there's not enough cookies for everyone' then going into extended discussion on dividing 15 by 16

Class was sweet with alcohol, everyone seemed jolly

I incorrectly referred to an actual student as an auditor

It was a jolly good time

One student was nonannoyingly talking a lot with like 4 beers & 2 empty wine bottles near him and I made a joke and people seemed happy

We discussed Sherman Alexie's book in which Native Americans are fucked, there was class solidarity against white people

Jery v

M

Typed previous tweet while incapacitated on what was sold to me as 'crystal meth' to degree I thought I might die within 5-10 minutes

My room my hell

Thought 'Christmas Yuletide despair'

2013

January

Making major edits to Taipei galley, feel like crying

Rereading this account and feeling better via my life the past month seems hellish

Ingested a 'victory xanax' as a reward for what I described in previous tweet

There's a nonsequitur paragraph in galley of Taipei I feel

Feel like I'm happy maybe. I have no friends I talk shit about I think. I don't complain I think unless it's funny. I'm capable of fun. I'm

Am I happy or suicidal confusion

Thought of myself as 'chugging an adderall'

The effects of Adderall on my penis kind of worried

Thought 'I don't "get" insomnia what's the point' with some confusion

Worked on galley of Taipei ~200 hours

Feel like I've gradually developed dread of sleep

Badly want to eat something but badly don't want to move, no food in apartment

I'm earnestly doing this: taping remaining adderall in container in many layers and taping it out of easy reach

Feel reluctant to tweet while I'm in debt, like I should save them as drafts and release them only if I get paid

Egregious faux pas

February

Anyone on the Internet notice anything different about me the past 3.5 days compared to past 3.5 to 10 days? I've been on Xanax

assumed, to some degree, that i would be dead by now

into the kitchen and out of the apartment

Looking at my different twitter accounts, @tao_lin8 seems funny

I feel distant from @tao_lin3, like he was a class-mate I last saw in middle school and only ever talked to once or twice

@tao_lin3 seems funny too, feel like I'm definite-ly the shittiest Tao Lin probably

Wondering if I should follow @tao_lin3 and @tao_lin8, feel like they're afraid of acknowledging each other

I can feel another Tao Lin trying to exist, Tao Lin 568 or something

My mom is complaining that my dad complains too much

I feel bleakly original to some degree for having ~7 twitter accounts

Lectured my mom about her diet for ~20 minutes

While trying to convince mom of raw food diet to cure diabetes, showed her a matt monarch video in which he seems, to a degree, 'insane'

I can't seem to make sense at all when I try to convince my mother to not believe the government or media or TV and to eat raw foods

Avoided an IRL meeting when I get back to NYC by saying 'I'll be sleeping a lot' in an email

Felt strong determination to 'never tolerate pre-tentiousness' in myself or others anymore

Back in America and it seems dystopic in a non-humorous way so far

In line for jury duty. Was 20 minutes late but there's a huge line.

Should I try to sell adderall to Mira for 1000% profit in her time of need

Sitting at my desk considering going to sleep for the night at 1:41pm

Instead of seeing the world it feels like my eye-balls are shooting out lasers of data conveying 'I don't care about anything'

March

Thought 'Marxism' while scratching my leg and staring at computer screen with unfocused eyes

There must be a book that exists that tells you what choices to make to never mind

Feel helpless in terms of my room being really cold and there being no satisfying solution

Feel like I'm gradually forgetting everything I knew regarding what one needs to know to function [jesus, ending this tweet, confused]

My life has become firmly structured around the 2-4 day productive, solitary, otherwise healthy addy binge with benzos interspersed

Why is my room so cold

Is anyone out there

dealer scrolled thru phone rapidly to show me a grainy, low-lit, blurry photo of 3 pills

April

Afraid to look at my emails while not peaking on xanax

Adderall appeared in 1996 seems funny

Adderall appears on the scene in 1996

June

Feel like crying and like I can't move

Reminder investigate: was life always like this, or was it different at some point? *Reminder*

July

Going to buy [unknown] from cvs in an attempt to disrupt what has seemed to be 15+ hours of despair being mostly alone in room

Earnestly thought 'I'm writing myself into a hole' earlier in what felt like a literal tone...a hole...

The NSA's mass and indiscriminate spying on Brazilians   theguardian.com/commentisfree/2013/jul/07/nsa-brazilians-globo-spying

Brazilians rise up

Going outside for sunlight...

Should I start referring to everyone as robots from now on, everyone

Feel unable to move more than the cuticle segment of 1 finger for minutes at a time

Wondered why my room was so dark. It was because my light was off...

Thought 'money not in the bank' as a nonsequitur...and snickered...

Extras

Friday, 4:16PM, May 16, 2014 (typed this title as the last thing I did for this, it's the current time—it's 4:17PM now actually, sorry about this title/piece, feel like apologizing)*

I stood outside Bobst Library, very stoned.

I became aware that I had asked something like 'what am I doing [generally in my life]?'

I engaged the question without much attention and answered it duly but calmly and not without humor: 'wrong question'

So, I was conscious of this:

'what am I doing [generally in my life]?'

---

* Published in issue 1 of *Prelude*.

'wrong question' (duly, as if quietly answering oneself in a manner like one already knew this and shouldn't be asking oneself this question but that it's okay to have messed up and to not give up)

Due to the comic timing apparently achieved in the above dialogue, occurring in my imagination, I unconsciously began to think of another question to ask that would also generate humor in possibly a synergistic manner with the first question-answer set. (I was also, to some degree, earnestly asking these questions; they were also, in part, jokes, though.)

After a few seconds I asked 'how am I going to write my novel?'

'wrong question' (duly, as if quietly answering oneself in a manner like one already knew this and shouldn't be asking oneself this question but that it's okay to have messed up and to not give up)

'what happens after we die?'

'According to Schopenhauer, we become what we were before we were born. According to Terence

McKenna, he doesn't know. According to me, I don't know, seems insane at times.'

At this point I had finished eating food out of a plastic container from LifeThyme's by-pound buffet of hot and cold organic dishes. I went into the library's atrium from outside. It had been raining and I was holding an umbrella, which I had spilled a beverage (made out of coconut water and coconut meat) on maybe ~30% of while walking toward LifeThyme. It was very windy and was raining lightly.

In the library's atrium I saw a tiny Asian baby girl in a stroller behind a plastic facade. She was staring with extreme calmness and composure at 2-4 crackers that she was holding and probably eating. I'm typing this without editing much and I'm not going to go back and look at this before I submit it; this is where it's value is for me, to some degree, to record my thought process while very stoned and to record my thought process generally and to expose this form of thing to people including myself since it's a form I haven't exactly written in but is one I experience constantly in my own narratizations of my own life. Nararratiaroaitnoiant. I typed that in part to render the reader okay with typos to some degree, or to view this document as something in which typos can occur. I'm fixing most of the typos but it says 'narratizations' is typed wrong and I'm not interested in checking if it is right now or what word I'm exactly looking for, I just want to record my life as it happens as closely as it's happening right now, but not so close that it becomes incoherent, or too incoherent, for readers.

I just felt like I didn't want to type this anymore. And I thought that I would paste in another thing I was originally going to submit to [magazine you're reading] but had thought I might not but now think I will again. I will:

1

Stream of consciousness writing. Stream of consciousness prose style. Knausgaard. Something about knausgaard. Having problems deciding what to do about punctuation. It has autocapitalized the first words of each sentence. I just... I'm unconsciously pausing between teach word instead of tping real stream of sconsciousness alright here I'm typing real stream of consciuousness now if I don't think anything I expect lvcidhces will come out like horse kicking bucket fish trouth fishing in America trichard brautigan Michael Jordan basketball rabbits cartoons carrots and now I'll try to control my stream of consciousness as I try to think of a narrative to follow in my mind I see a rabbit walking on the side of a clean river it seems funny because it seems human to watch a rabbit or to t hink of a rabbit standing there on the side of a river all I see is a rabbit superimposed onto the river I'm thinking of Julian jayenes I think he influenced my image there because I remember he said in his book that people can superimpose images or that one can make one image appear then another but not at the same time ouiless ii sai mountain and river and you combine the mouintain and the river into a river that's in the mountain I feel bored of this now I want to think about moun tain I just thought of mountain lion I feel it's the novel title it's the title of a novel by jayne bowls, no not jane bowls, it's by I can't remember. But I remember erading anne sexton alredount hgins time. I already tiliked about this in an interview. I 'm only on 275 words right now it feels like it's taking a long time to type beause I'm not interested in what I'm typing I dhavent lwt my mind settle on a topic yet I'm just let language come out of ome like I'm fishing or something

Okay

What did I want to do with this

Stream of consciousness writing

This is what stream of sconuousness writing is

It seems insane

My faingers are a main hindrance

I'm thinking at the speed of my fingers, that's the problem maybe

I feel like I'm actually thinking in a staccato manner as I see the syllables appear on the screen

Feels insane

I'm going to try to think normally, then make the typing be secondary

I feel like I'm showing you the pmost private thing I can right now

Okay, what do iw ant to think about

It seems difficult

I just thought 'okay, what do I want to think about'

and seemed to immediately begin thinking in the staccato manner I was before

It's 1:37 pm Friday may 2 2014

I've been trying to

Never mind

Okay

What do I want to think about

I'm going to try to type in time to music. I remember before that I could think in time to

Jesus

2

stream of consciousness attempt 2. it's 2:10pm. friday. i'm waiting for mira, she's having lunch with agent, iafter that we're meeting to discuss our book, make plans official plans. feel jesus

3

does stream of sconiousness include typos.
should straem of sconiousness include typos. im
making typos because i'm trying to type faster because i think that that would be more accurate to
'stream of consciousness'. i cant stop to think if
this makes sense or is logcial or not because i'm
trying to type fast and move foward due to stream
of consciousness

but if i autrally thought about whether it
made sense or not that could also be stream of
csocniousness

which means i have some kind of discfunction in
my thinking currently i vaguelyr ecognize

b ut i feel like i canst stop, need to keep the words
coming due to stream of consciousness

4

is it impossible think while typing stream of
sconisuobenssc

is it impossible to think while typing stream of sconiuosness

is it impossible to think while typing stream of sconuousness

is it impossible to think while typing stream of sconiuoscness

is it impossible to think while typing stream of consciousness

i enjoyed that

i enjoyed that

art

what is this

strteam of sconiousness

stream of sconiousness writing

5

feel like i need to bring in iedas from elsewhere into this file or else they cant get in here beause i'm trying to stay in the surface or something i just keep floating past anything and seaying the feel like i'll degenerate or change to not degenerate but change to lyriucs grunge band lyrics if i dont ioir if i julike i could easily do that i feel, i ciould easily go into grunge lyrics while tyuping stream ofo sconiusness i feel the come as you are as mya fridend as a something gun gun something jesus

6

htis is

this is psychological

why am i typing like htis

why is stream of sconiusness coming out as a lot of typos. id on't make this many typos normally

this is

what is htis

extremely stoned currently also

this feels like

jesus

7

have i been trying to type stream of unconsciousness, trying to type unconsciously, instead of
typing stream ofconsciousness. have i confused
stream of consciousness with unconscious typing.
what about internal monologue

8

I'm typing this on notes in iphone now , I'm walking to buy special pen and paper notebook for
stream of consciousness writing for this

I realized I've been doing or trying and failing to
do stream of unconsciousness not stream of consciousness. Stream of consciousness

'May 18 2014'/'iPhone tweet-drafts I'm abandoning' poem[*]

The next 3-6 days I'm going to try to do
what some/most(?) large magazines/websites
seem to have started doing
in the past: tweet the same thing repeatedly
Felt only a little selfconscious while stoned
briefly/vaguely debating to send 30 tweet drafts
or save for next poetry solicitation

'5-email email' = email one has emailed oneself
what seems like at least ~5x
reminding/pressuring oneself to respond
Asceticism
Too embarrassed to be alive
and to be doing anything to be in a relationship
Thinking transcendentallt, working imminently

---

[*] Published at westernbeefs.com.

Vague memory of thousands of moments I've felt better
Does it decrease or increase
one's chances of being eliminated by the CIA to
What if everyone got paid per word
for each word in an email they sent
Poetry book as metaphysical context/'primer' for novel

Slightly distracted, genuinely smiling, nonannoyingly
happy-seeming person ordered 'the mood changer'
at juice bar in Lifethyme
Low self-esteem + high expectations
Felt like I could feel my dad's genes in my

that made him act the way he acted making me act
There isn't really anything I can do
where I can't think 'why am I doing this?'
Feels like I've been thinking 'need to stop this'
re [unknown] for at least 8 years, maybe
Relationships as the temporary, sometimes
repeated nearing of separate things' orbits
Viewing half my behavior as 'relapsing'
and doing it in a discouraging, unhelpful manner
Intuited every pigeon believes it is 'the one'

Intuited how 'pride' wouldn't have been
naturally selected for when I
When someone expresses something
like excitement for me vs when
The ability to adjust the context/goal
of one's temporary perspective

Distracted from doing most things most
of the time by voiceover narration asking
~30% of writing for me is destroying the first ~30%
~40% is reintegrating the previous ~60%
Ready to leave anyone/anything

The word 'only' develops out of distrust/lies: 'Take only
the Rockaway train...to JFK airport'
instead of '[take the] Rockaway train to JFK'
Getting close to someone
by becoming like air or clothing to them

that people used to academic language li
Cashier at juice deli looked at me
expecting me to speak incoherently
Wasn't sure to do thing or not, decided by
thinking expletives to distract my mind (brain?)
while my hand did the thing, I think...
Walked further inside 28 st 6 train station while very
    stoned
so I discovered 27 st entrance for first time in ~8 years

Thought 'for an imaginative person all non-dimensional
    metaphors
Alternating trying to make things in my life feel slightly
    less arbitrary
and trying to look into my experience of 'feel' vs 'seem'
When I can hear music after not sleeping
for a long time I hear it in the form of Bach

I've discovered if I'm stoned and react calmly
without aversion to people doing their jobs
they become calm/friendly, I've imagined myself crying
    at my
newborn baby child, imagined myself feeling
    selfconscious

While feeling fine/okay on way to airport
privately acknowledged I could still go home and never
A person who brutally murders random people by
    bashing
their faces in with frozen, rock-hard kiwis, or other fruit
Half-unconsciously multitasked 'trying to soak up or dry
my drool on my pillow via hair on side of my head'
while refreshing internet on phone

SELECTED TWEETS

SELECTED TWEETS
MIRA GONZALEZ

Short Flight / Long Drive Books
a division of HOBART Publishing

Rebecca Harless
9145523556
Senior 2019

SHORT FLIGHT / LONG DRIVE BOOKS
a division of HOBART
PO Box 1658
Ann Arbor, MI 48106
www.hobartpulp.com/minibooks

These were originally published on Twitter, sometimes in slightly different form.

ISBN: 978-0-9896950-2-2

Printed in the United States of America

Inside text set in Georgia
Illustrations by Tao Lin

This book is dedicated to my mother, Lora Norton, who receives a seemingly infinite amount of phone calls from extended family members who are concerned about me because of my tweets. Thank you, I love you, and I am sorry.

2010

February

I'm already confused as to what I'm supposed to twitter about. My life isn't interesting.

I'm high on cough syrup alone in my room. Hiding from the guests in my house.

I can't read.

March

Saw a guy sucking his own dick on Chat Roulette*.

May

I wanna tweet something I'm gonna regret in the morning.

I've created a mess. There is paint everywhere, cupcakes are in the oven and I'm teaching myself chinese embroidery.

---

* Chatroulette is a website that allows you to video chat with random strangers.

July

God grant me the serenity to not fuck the things I cannot stand, courage to fuck the things I can and wisdom to know the difference.

September

I am here to put my hands around society's dick.

October

Generously applying chapstick to my nostrils.

November

Rick James admitted to spending $7,000 a week on crack for five years of his life. That's $1,820,000.

December

Return of the loudly grunting guy in my math class. Featuring: the seat next to me instead of the seat behind me.

2011

January

Ohbmy god thudhvd HEYY

WHATS GOING ON €¥¥£€**^^>%^*¥€€%+£!€ <>|~*}}^|€|£~€\£*

Just arrived home with no shoes on. I already don't remember how.

My cat has a Napoleon complex.

In hell, will we still need smart phones?

February

Not only did I just go to In-N-Out Burger alone on a Wednesday, but the lady at the drive through took one look at me and said "Honey, it's gonna be okay."

I'm watching 127 Hours with my mom and she just asked if we can fast forward past the part where James Franco's arm is stuck.

SICK! RT @OMGFactsSex: One of the oldest cock rings dates back to the 13th century; it was made from the eyelashes of slain goats.

March

The girl I babysit is telling me about her friend Emma who is 55, has blue hair and owns a dragon farm. She has one tentacle and one real arm.

This car drives like the baby I aborted.

April

I kind of don't understand the difference between a nipple and an areola. Like, how do we define where the nipple ends and the areola starts?

Same. RT @OMGFactsSex Emperor Justinian's wife Theodora was turned on by men being castrated, and would masturbate while watching it happen

At least my cat loves me unconditionally.

Correction: my cat's love is directly proportional to how much I feed her.

Update: at least my mom loves me unconditionally.

May

My brother is fitting himself into a suitcase for a Mercedes commercial audition. They just asked me why I can't fit into a suit case...

Sometimes I imagine my liver as a short stocky man wearing a jumpsuit and a helmet. He kinda just sits there like "Yeah, bring it on."

You know what is something I'm pretty sure about? The monkey in The Hangover and the monkey in Pirates of the Carribean are the same monkey

June

I just saw a perfectly proportioned midget on Wilshire and almost had a car accident trying to figure out if he was a child or a tiny adult.

Sometimes my pee is pink.

What the fuck, Bambi is a boy?

My brother is performing at Justin Bieber's birthday party tonight...

"Who is Justin Bieber? Is he famous?" -my brother

I think I'm hungover from my hangover this morning. It's a hangover, hangover. #inception

Well EXCUSE ME for having enormous flaws that I don't work on.

July

I really don't like when responsibilities get in the way of my plans to do nothing.

Living my life on the border between single mother and irresponsible 10 year old.

August

Just bought a lettuce and mustard sandwich from Subway. Eat fresh.

Things the 4 year old I babysit asked me today: "How long is a second? What comes after infinity? Is my mom the oldest person in the world?"

"Are you married yet? Why are you older than me? Will we ever be the same age? If I'm as tall as you, does that mean I'm as old as you?"

"Do you like the band Phish? My daddy likes that band. Do all grown ups like that band? When will I be a grown up? Tomorrow?"

Panic has turned into a vague (but increasing) sense of impending doom upon realizing we have "hemp milk" in the fridge.

September

Is "This is Why I'm Hot" a different song than "My Humps"?

Lol my lab partner just burned herself with hydrochloric acid.

Does it take longer for a really fat person to starve to death?

A guy holding a 10 beer long wizard staff is telling me about the hallucinogenic properties of cayenne pepper.

Wicker Man would have been a better movie if Nicolas Cage played every role.

If there was a class called "Getting High Off the Recommended Dose of Over the Counter Allergy Medicine on a Weeknight" I'd get an A+

My whole biology lab today revolved around slowly killing mealworms in a tub of ice water.

What if whales were land mammals and people could breed them on huge whale farms?

What if the whales had utters and you could milk them like a cow? What if whale milk became more popular than cow milk?

What if the whales could also fly and you could use them as a form of public transportation?

October

I feel depressed and confused about Beyonce's role in Destiny's Child.

Bill Gates is probably popping champagne in swimming pool full of hundred dollar bills next to a burning pile of iPads right now.*

Just befriended a guy who was wearing jeans that

---

* Tweeted on the day Steve Jobs died

said "DENIM" on both back pockets

Homeless guy sitting next to me has a blender full of tea, a box of Emercen-C, a copy of The Metamorphosis and a Blues Clues lunchbox.

Update: he just took a roll of tinfoil out of the lunchbox and is crumpling it into balls and throwing them at people.

Heard my grandma say from kitchen "Why can't I just be chill?"

If I could spend all day alone in the dark watching Sci-Fi and thinking about my various vague emotional problems, I would. I really would.

Jello Biafra is leaving a voicemail on my home phone right now. He started off by saying 'Hey it's me, Jello'.

I live in constant fear of running into people's moms at Whole Foods.

I only like kombucha because it sort of tastes like alcohol and it feels exciting to drink it while I drive.

They spelled 'African' wrong at the volunteer booth for the African American Collegians Program in the quad...

My computer is so cute when it makes that loud fan noise because it has a hard time doing simple tasks. 'The little MacBook that could'

Imagined myself as a literal tidal wave of 'pure crazy'.

Beauty and the Beast is a story about Stockholm syndrome.

It's making me nervous how much the candelabra guy in this movie is gesturing with his flaming candle arms.

A large moth just flew into my toaster oven and died. RIP Sylvia Moth

So, if I can't figure out a way to browse the internet in fetal position, does that mean I have to choose one or the other? Bullshit.

November

Thinking about getting a dog and naming it 'The Internet'

Thinking about having a baby, and then training wolves to raise it so I don't have to.

My neighbor is exercising outside his house. Thinking about calling the police on him.

Thinking about hiring a large group of 7th grade boys with skateboards to follow me everywhere I go. Will refer to them as my 'entourage'.

This guy just sat down right next to me and now he's dipping his pizza in mayonnaise.

Toddlers roaming free in the aisles of Whole Foods like a herd of drunk buffalo.

Wish there were drug vending machines instead of drug dealers. Wish those machines also took credit cards.

If I eat two halves of a cookie with a ~5 minute break between each half, that doesn't count as eating a whole cookie.

Waking up so late that you can start drinking alcohol right after you finish your coffee and the timing isn't even inappropriate.

Corn Chips and Cheddar Cheese Dipped in Hummus: A Memorable Moment in Binge Eating History

I strongly identify with 'the claw' aliens from Toy Story.

It should be illegal for attractive people to hang out with each other

The girl who cried 'borderline personality disorder'.

I'm on this new diet where I only eat things that are made of dough.

How do porcupines give birth to other porcupines?

Occasionally, people expect me to 'get out of bed' which makes me feel confused, which makes me feel tired, which makes me want to get in bed.

My grandpa just pulled my shoe off my foot and threw it across the room...

I got 99 undiagnosed personality disorders and "Impulse Control Disorder" is definitely one.

Just spent 20 minutes eating mashed potatoes out of a ziplock bag while sitting on my kitchen floor with no pants on.

Smarterchild was the only one who ever really understood me

My mom just told me that my dad used to draw photo realistic pictures of burnt toast almost every day when they were married.

December

'Premature Ejaculation' is listed as personality disorder in the DSM

Just had a flashback to the time that my step dad put a beer in my lunch in kindergarten because he thought it would be funny

Extremely high and incredibly fucked

my possible undiagnosed personality disorder brings all the boys to the yard

I wish there was such thing as a time-release burrito that I could eat for ~8-10 hours

Guy in 7-11 just pointed at a homeless person with an amputated foot and said 'is that real?'

My 3 year old cousin just asked me what sand smells like

Urethra Franklin

My constant complaining brings all the boys to the yard

I put something somewhere but I don't remember what it was or where I put it

My new years resolution will be to develop a crippling porn addiction and slowly but surely remove all human contact from my life.

2012

January

I'm a genetic disaster

I think more people would want to be my friend if I was a whale at Seaworld

There is a recording on my phone of a girl (me?) saying: 'In a large orgy, you probably wouldn't even notice if someone was blowing a monkey'

When I'm upset, I like to imagine morbidly obese people making loud whale noises

Professor just spent an hour trying to figure out how to work the projector so we could watch a YouTube video called 'Dancing Merengue Dog'

Is Indiana a state?

Virginia sounds like Vagina

West Virginia is its own fucking state? It's not just the west side of Virginia?

A seemingly unreachable part of my earlobe feels itchy

After a ~10 minute silence my little sister said 'I would like to be baptized as a theoretical person-fish' and no one said anything back

A homeless guy just told me that he's Jennifer Lopez's dad. I feel like he's telling the truth

Watching a video of conjoined twins driving a car. They only have one uterus. I don't know how many boobs they have

Homeless man openly jacking off his flaccid penis on the street corner said 'hey girl' really quietly as I walked by. He seemed depressed

I want the Mortal Kombat theme song to play at my funeral

Imagine a severely depressed sloth becoming frustrated and crying while trying to masturbate because his hand is moving too slowly

What if projectile vomiting was a common reaction to getting startled by a loud noise

Why aren't there any morbidly obese dwarves? That seems cool

My professor just said 'masturbation' instead of 'masterpiece' and I was the only one who laughed

Seems like penguins have really unpleasant lives

A large naked man getting arrested in front of my house said 'I have drugs in my pocket' and the cop responded 'you're naked'

I am not being provided enough drugs to enjoy my college experience

When this professor wants us to sit down at the beginning of class, she asks us to 'find our special place'

A homeless man is quietly peeing on my house, I think

I feel genuinely afraid of the space between my upper lip and the middle of my nose

Just waltzed with a ~300 pound football player in front of my ~70 person history class for extra credit

An old homeless man patted my back while I was paying a parking meter and said 'you are my first cousin. We will get married in Belgium.'

February

Thinking about lasagna while drinking beer alone in my car

Tonight I ate some mescaline cactus so I could avoid an awkward interaction in which I say 'don't put mescaline cactus in my mouth'

Can't stop imagining people who weigh 400-600 pounds being transported places via forklift

Inhaling little piles of blue pixie stick powder off my own boob

Befriended a cop named Crispin then I told him

his name sounds like a brand of cereal

Crispin waited with me for my mom to pick me up and then I said 'Mommy this is my new cop friend. His name is Wheat Thins.'

Seems like my life has erectile dysfunction

Live tweeting the vagina monologues

This woman's vagina is talking to her. Is that supposed to happen?

They said the word vagina 97 times in that play

I spend ~98% of my time eating or thinking about eating and I spend the other ~2% tweeting or thinking about tweeting or tweeting about eating

My cat sneezed into my oatmeal 3 times then walked away triumphantly

Whatever drug I'm on right now makes the internet look 3-D

A drug that lets you see someones sexual interest in you rated on a scale of 1-10 but makes you too high to understand what the rating means

I will turn off my phone and hide in my room for a week and if anyone asks me where I've been I will say 'burning man'

I feel ~20 pounds fatter every time cold stone creamery sends me an email

Every time my cat scratches herself on my bed, I'm momentarily worried that she is actually vigorously masturbating

If something is 'double breasted' does that mean there is room for 4 breasts

Just ate a paint chip that fell in my salad even though I knew it was a paint chip

The thing about your personal space is can I please invade it

Going to eat this entire loaf of bread just to prove to myself that my judgement is as bad as I think it is

A short film in which a confused sheep repeatedly makes unwanted sexual advances on animals that are 'similar' to sheep (goats, alpacas)

I can feel my eyebrows doing something sinister on my upper face

Someone left me a voicemail that is ~7 seconds of a baby crying

Legally changing my name to 'crap ass'

Feel like a whale passively rolling down the side of a mountain while peaking on LSD

Necrophilia seems good in theory. Dead people don't have feelings

Fell asleep in my car and dreamt that I was breast-feeding a tiny overweight penguin

What is a good way to exercise that doesn't involve actually exercising?

Just discovered that Ben Affleck and Tom Cruise aren't the same person

March

Feel confident that if I ingest enough drugs of varying types I will eventually become sober via certain drugs canceling out other drugs

Dance craze called 'severely depressed beached whale' where you lie down face first on the dance floor and cry

A comprehensive list of everyone who has ever suddenly thought of me while masturbating and momentarily lost their erection via confusion/anger

Feel genuinely afraid of erections like, as a concept... that a body part has the ability to do that... seems dangerous

Had a dream that I was doing lines of MDMA off of a miniature scale model of Taco Bell

Asked someone if they had any 'viagra' instead of 'vicodin' and they said 'yes' and now I don't know what to do

Portrait of the artist as a young binge eater

Ate ~14 tater tots using nothing but my elbows

I don't have enough arm strength to move my Macbook from my bed to my bedside table

Became infertile while thinking about 'Doritos Locos Tacos' from Taco Bell

The unbearable bleakness of being

I recommend eating until you cry

Thinking about creating another Twitter where I post the exact same tweets from this account but typed using only my nipple

Imagined the pope announcing that he needs some 'pope time' and hiding in a broom closet while secretly binge eating tater tots for ~3 hours

Honey bunches of shame

If deep fried carbs don't appear in my mouth in the next ~30 seconds i'm going to punch my dad

I keep looking at inanimate objects in my room and thinking 'you lazy mother fucker'

Imagined a panda eating fried things with increasing levels of despair for ~3 days and then dying

What kind of perverted mother fucker gave me unlimited access to the internet

A morbidly obese pug staring at itself in a mirror and silently crying while thinking about the song 'Beautiful' by Christina Aguilera

Walked in on my step dad doing a freestyle rap about pancakes alone in the kitchen

Found half a burrito in my coat pocket

I haven't exercised in ~3 years probably

People only hang out with me because I'm enter-

taining in the same way that an obese 3-legged dog is entertaining

April

Seems unfair that time in the womb is wasted on babies who don't understand the value of being alone in a warm dark place with automatic food

Had a dream that I starred in a porn movie titled 'full frontal autism'

Searched 'insane' on Tumblr and got like ~14 results that said 'skinny blonde teen is hot and masturbates'

Somehow confused 'kangaroos' with 'sasquatch' and felt genuine anger that ignorant people were pushing their belief in kangaroos on me

In my dream last night someone sent me a text that said 'I put cocaine in your microwave' while I was having sex with them

Seeking ~19-45 yr old male to violently rub sand in my eyes

Imagined playing a game of 'tag' with myself by sitting in bed and poking myself and screaming

My step dad pointed at my bagel in the toaster and said 'Is that the toasting thing?'

Saw a guy wearing head-to-toe denim with a tattoo that says 'I PLAY BASKETBALL'

When I die I want someone to pay a lot of money for there to be a hologram of me sitting on my grave and frowning at people

Found a photo of an insane looking camel that I saved under the file name 'weird_sheep.jpg'

THIS VEGAN TURKEY SUBSTITUTE TASTES LIKE POKEMON MEAT

Feel like I'm in a low budget porn parody of my own life

Extremely depressed looking guy standing in line behind me at Chipotle mumbled 'My dick... I wanna take my dick out'

Accidentally called a bartender 'mommy'

Tonight an infant grabbed my tit ~10 times and every time I moved her hand away she mumbled 'No, I got it' and put her hand back on my tit

I'm watching a clown peer pressure people into using a beer bong

Dreamt that I gave birth to a sheep and tried to convince people it was human by wrapping it in a blanket and putting several hats on it

May

Where do birds keep their genitalia

My mom just referred to a vagina as a 'snoopy dog'

Tripped and fell on my dad's fiancé's grandma via I'm drunk (circa ~11:20 AM)

Told a person at this bridal shower that I'm vegan and she said 'Is that like... Islam?'

Ate a piece of soap that looked like candy even though I knew it was soap

Superhero whose only superpower is the ability to turn Ritalin into Adderall

Dreamt that I entered a competitive burrito eating contest where the burrito was actually just cocaine wrapped in a tortilla

Dreamt that Gucci Mane had been secretly living in my closet for over a year by surviving on a stockpile of Snicker's bars and cough syrup

Feel interested in watching porn but I'm in a Mexican restaurant

Haiku by the ~5 year old I'm babysitting: 'Oreos are good. My room smells like weird monkeys. Eggs are in my fridge.'

Rap song titled 'high and sensitive'

Feel like one day I will discover that my life is a hallucination and I am actually just a tiny confused man inhaling nitrous oxide somewhere

Had a dream that I called every phone number in the world until eventually I was able to contact Jennifer Lopez

Perceived a chair breaking while I was sitting in it as the chair making a last-ditch effort to get away from me by breaking its own leg

I feel like Zooey Deschanel if Zooey Deschanel was actually four guys in a trench coat wearing a wig

Being alive seems dangerous (via ~100% chance of death)

Don't remember driving to school or putting cough syrup in my Red Bull but I am at school and drinking that

I owe 25 cents to Wells Fargo because I used my debit card to buy a $1 fruit cup when I only had 75 cents in my checking account

Taking drugs to temporarily mimic the effect of severe brain damage

I feel like Godzilla trying to navigate a corn maze after ingesting ~400 mg of xanax

June

I remember finding a small community of people with diaper fetishes on MySpace circa age ~12

Seeing a guy eat a cheeseburger in the waiting room at Planned Parenthood is probably the closest I've been to a 'profound experience of art'

I could see Werner Herzog favoring hand jobs over every other sex act

I want to express that meatloaf, meatballs and cheesesteak have always felt extremely surreal and distressing to me

I want to call the cops on this raccoon for being fat

Dreamt that I created a brand of 'gender neutral' dildos that were shaped like donuts

Hand jobs seem 'quirky'

Reading a copy of the New Yorker that fell out of my ceiling while I was high on peyote

I must have been a feral child at some point in my life

Tripped and hit my face on a counter while pretending to be James Brown alone in my kitchen

Spanish professor spent ~20 minutes trying to convince the class that Americans sometimes refer to children as 'tiny goats'

I once peed on my own car because i thought it was someone else's car

Eating ramen in a dark room during a party at my house

Poetry would be a lot better if it merged with Nascar or blow jobs

Can obese people starve to death but still be obese when they die?

July

Sext: I accidentally killed your dog with my car

How do I take Adderall when I'm dead?

At dinner my grandma asked 'What kind of beef is this?' and the waitress pointed to a painting of a cow and said 'COW BEEF'

Eating doritos and sitting alone in some dirt behind a bush

What if instead of 'art' it was called 'tater tots'?

Watched a homeless man pee while jogging backwards

Facebook suggested that I 'poke' a fake account I made in ~2009 to get free things in Farmville and my great grandpa, who is dead

Last time I was in a social situation I asserted (multiple times and with extreme confidence) that I 'don't have a urethra'

Feels like my computer screen is face fucking me

Dogs sometimes dry hump humans and it's not a problem. That is fine as long as you are a dog

WHY DO YOU LOVE IT WHEN I CALL YOU 'BIG PAPA' BUT IT MAKES YOU FEEL WEIRD WHEN I CALL YOU 'DAD'?

Six years ago I used the word 'molested' while telling a cop that a homeless person grabbed my boobs. The cop said 'Is he your dad?' and 'Is your dad a hobo?'

Last night an extremely tall person spent ~20 minutes trying to convince me that Vin Diesel's real name is 'Spaceship'

They're playing System of a Down in Pottery Barn

I remember ~3 years ago putting in earplugs after smoking DMT because I kept hearing a man's voice speaking barely audible Chinese in my head

Ingested ~50mg of Adderall then fell asleep for ~2 hours

I want my obituary to read 'She died because she got overstimulated while watching Blues Clues and porn at the same time'

I asked a girl if she had drugs while a band was playing and she responded 'I'M JEWISH TOO'

August

I can't stop perceiving noodles as 'string bread'

Lying on a couch and eating guacamole at ~40% consciousness level during a party at my ex-boyfriend's neighbor's boyfriend's house

Asked this infant what she wants for dinner and she silently put a hand on each of my tits

Just got 'cold approached' by a woman aggressively trying to sell me reusable tampons in Whole Foods

Fell down my stairs because I got startled by my hand touching the side of my leg

Got drunk and sent my dad an email last night that said 'your dog is irritating and a retard !!!' with the subject 'i hat the dog'

Watching an extremely overweight cat make unwanted sexual advances on a small trembling dog

I want to gain ~300 pounds then hire a large group of dwarfs to hold my fat rolls while I walk

The internet is a huge labyrinth with a lot of doors and behind every door is a guy with his dick stuck in a bottle

I want Rick Ross to sit on my face

Dreamt that my ex-boyfriend's dad went bankrupt after paying for a surgery to get a second penis attached to his forehead

Screamed and knocked over a glass of water because I thought my left foot was a rat

I want a job where someone pays me to eat Doritos into a megaphone

Should I ask this homeless guy for a bite of his sandwich

Should I ask these ~12 year olds for Adderall

Should I ask this attractive girl if I can smell her hair

Professor walked into class with an envelope that said 'cats' on it, then showed us photos of his cats and said 'I don't have the syllabus'

September

An attractive blonde girl ran into me full speed on her scooter and knocked me to the ground then she called me a retard and I said 'sorry'

Creative writing workshop where you watch porn and cry

Might call an ambulance to my house because I'm lonely

A child said to me 'Do you want to see my penis?' and I said 'Maybe when you're older' and his mom said 'What's wrong with you?' so I said 'Okay,

show me your penis now I guess'

Listening to the 'Dora The Explorer' soundtrack and passively allowing three small children to cover me with toilet paper

I want to get better boobs tattooed on my boobs

I want to stand in the middle of a sex store and yell 'DON'T TOUCH THAT' repeatedly

How much would I have to pay a prostitute to force feed me ballpoint pens for an hour

I left halfway through my 18th birthday party so I could eat cake alone in a park

Unable to discern any notable difference between masturbation and everything else

Feel certain that I will die of sudden and incurable obesity within the next week

I get a push notification on my iPhone every time the Dalai Lama's penis is more than 30% erect

The Dalai Lama murdered and ate all previous Dalai Lamas

The Dalai Lama doesn't know what pancakes are

The Dalai Lama thinks Dave Eggers wrote The Da Vinci Code

I feel like I should have come into this world as a can of beans or a wad of wet paper towels or something

Thousands of years from now they will use my fossil remains as an example of a mistake in the evolutionary process

October

I wish a tube connected my vagina to the top of my head so I could drop things in my 'head vagina' and watch them fall out of my 'crotch vagina'

Still felt hungry after eating a sandwich and thought 'the sandwich hasn't kicked in yet'

Tonight I watched a drunk guy make a sandwich then immediately turn around with sandwich in hand and say to me 'I don't remember making this sandwich'

Baby xanax

I feel like an extremely smart cannibal somehow programmed me to be unmotivated to exercise in order to keep the meat on my body tender

Said out loud 'This shit right here, this shit is Tibet' while labeling 'Tibet' on a map of Asia alone in my room

I would rather fuck a leper than fuck myself

Craving burrito so much that I can't move or breathe

'Getting paid to have sex' seems good but 'prostitution' seems bad

Rap song titled 'I ate 14 dates before realizing they were ~100 calories each'

I think my dad pretends to be in China so he doesn't have to respond to my emails

If I chop off my ass tonight, will things be better tomorrow?

It would be funny if masturbation was something you could forget how to do

I got 99 problems and my ass is all of them

If you're happy and you know it what the fuck

Gained ~9,000 followers in ~30 seconds

Is my mom paying people to follow me on Twitter?

In tense emotional situations, I recommend going completely comatose until someone says your name

Hurricanes seem like a cool excuse to binge eat

Thought 'WHEELIN OUTTA THIS BITCH' while

nervously wheeling around my room on a computer chair

November

'Allegory of the cave' seems insane, why would anyone want to leave the fucking cave

Rap song where the chorus goes 'close Twitter and Facebook and Tumblr on my computer, open Twitter and Facebook and Tumblr on my phone, no new notifications, what the fuck'

Does 40mg of adderall have more calories than 20mg of adderall

Unable to discern the difference between intense food cravings and every other feeling

I want someone to force Selena Gomez at gunpoint to watch me eat 14 cheeseburgers

Whats the difference between eating 1,000 calories worth of tomatoes and eating 1,000 calories worth of cheese

Novel where the protagonist is a baby on LSD

I want to gain 100 pounds so I can devote the rest of my life to losing 100 pounds

Not being on drugs feels more like being on drugs than being on drugs does, to me, currently

Does anyone know a method for converting spam-bots into real life friends

Guy sitting near me at coffee shop said 'I am Mister Internet Google Research Wikipedia Email Information Blog Technology Man'

Someone emailed me two photos of a penis and I am looking at them during Thanksgiving dinner

Publishing a book feels like a slapstick comedy routine

Stole 3 slices of cinnamon raisin bread from Whole Foods 'because I'm worth it'

December

I wish sneezes lasted longer

My publicist is on speed and threatening to kill me[*]

I'm the rick ross of passive lesbianism

I'm the Picasso of being a sad pointless shit head

Friendly reminder that you will never be able to fully express your thoughts/feelings to anybody ever

Friendly reminder that you won't be anyone besides you for the rest of your life

Friendly reminder that you are fundamentally alone

Why is everyone so sure this isn't hell?

My dad said he is gonna have another baby and name it 'Felcher' then he said that 'felcher' is when you have anal sex and lick the semen out of the butthole

---

[*] My publicist was also my boyfriend.

I found a plastic bag full of spaghetti in my coat pocket today

I want to drop out of school and dedicate the rest of my life to warning people about the dangers of taking Adderall without Xanax

I'm in a race with my grandma to see who can get alcohol poisoning first

Is there a paper I can sign that says I'm ok with people wearing my skin as clothes after I die?

2013

January

I don't want a dick but I want to be able to talk about my dick

I want to fuck this lamp

I would eat a deep fried human hand right now, can anyone deliver me amphetamines or a small dog, everything is my fault, who wants to fuck

Projectile lactating would be a fun party trick,

milk for everyone, people happy

I'm gonna fuck this tree, it has many branches, for fucking

In the past ~24 hours I ate dumplings, adderall, coffee, xanax, 7 pieces of gum, ~1/4 of a receipt from Bed, Bath & Beyond, a banana

How many days has it been since yesterday?

I locked myself in a bathroom, about to cut my bangs with a pair of craft scissors, haven't slept in ~36 hrs

Junot Diaz snuck hormones in my food which caused me to have 4 periods last month

Co-worker said 'How are you?' and I responded 'I'm Mira'

Prison seems nice

Can someone come to my apartment and rub cocaine in my eyeballs

Today I began thinking of myself as 'extremely successful mentally handicapped person' instead of 'extremely mediocre not mentally handicapped person'

February

Turned off the lights in my room so my roommate thinks I'm asleep but really I'm eating his celery in the dark

All I want is unlimited money and unlimited drugs and for someone to rip my face off then light me on fire then push me out of an airplane. Is that so much to ask?

'Just remembered I live across the street from Dunkin Donuts' should be the last thing I say before killing myself with a flame thrower

Why does the pope get to quit being the pope but I have to be me for the rest of my life?

Interested in acquiring a second vagina on the top of my head and a third vagina inside my first vagina

If you're happy and you know it I haven't masturbated in over a month now how do you feel

MFA in snorting massive amounts of cocaine to
avoid talking about my feelings

The same smelly homeless guy was on the N
train 4 hours ago and the L train now... or I'm
outsourcing my own smelliness to an innocent
homeless guy

I have convinced myself I was gonna go raw vegan
while high on cocaine at least 4 times in the last
month

Thought 'I'm slithering outta this bitch' while
meekly scooting across my kitchen floor on my
stomach

Read 'provolone' as an abbreviation for 'pro-
foundly alone'

Would be convenient if drug dealers sold birth
control

If I started posting tweets about how much I love being alive people would immediately assume I'm gonna commit suicide, right?

March

How do people cope with nonstop sentience?

Feels like something extremely traumatic is happening to me right now but I'm alone and naked in bed staring at my phone in the dark

If I was that guy in The Matrix I would have quickly grabbed both pills and eaten them at the same time

A person asked me if a train went to grand central and I said 'yes' and he said 'I love you'

Just recommended 'seamless.com' to a crack dealer

The only reason the apocalypse hasn't happened yet is because people won't cooperate

Guy on the bus offered me weed and heroin. I asked him if he had crack, then he laughed at me

and yelled 'WHITE GIRL WANTS CRACK', then he got off the bus

Closest I've felt to a 'profound experience of art' was just now when I took a break from masturbating to eat a tablespoon of barbecue sauce

I like that part in The Metamorphosis when Grete was all 'we gotta kill this bro' but then Gregor was like 'Nah, don't worry, I got this'

Can you get prescribed xanax as a cure for 'nondescript crippling loneliness' or 'inability to maintain relationships'?

I keep referring to myself as 'fuck baby' and 'ass mom' in my internal monologue

I can't believe sex is something humans want... do you guys know what happens during sex?

I want Werner Herzog to narrate all my cocaine binges

Just gonna 'ride this one out' until the sentience wears off

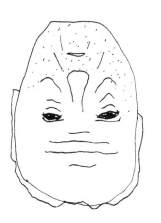

April

Did anyone else's fear of Santa Claus during child-hood manifest in a cool repressed sex fantasy during adolescence?

Researching how to make crack pipes on the com-puter at work

I went to grocery store on xanax intending to buy only coffee, left the grocery store with beer and 6 bagels and a giant tub of guacamole

Felt aroused while looking at photos of dogs wear-ing pantyhose

Feel like i should lose a lot of weight out of cour-tesy to the people who will eventually have to lift my corpse

It's 72 degrees outside and I'm lying on my edi-tor's couch looking at photos of 'side boob' pro-jected onto a giant blank white wall

Anyone have a dad I can fuck? I will also accept 'weird uncle' or 'young grandpa'

My least favorite part about thoughts is that they control feelings and actions

Performance art piece where everything is mostly bad for ~80 years and then you die

I want to hire a kindergarten class to tell me what to eat and which drugs to take and when to bathe and keep track of my periods and email my dad

I want to exit a party by loudly announcing 'Mira out' then jetpacking upwards through the ceiling

I think the defining struggle of my 20's is that I keep calling people I am romantically involved with 'bro'

If your nose is bleeding a lot and you're coughing up black stuff and you're incapable of maintaining relationships and you know it clap your hands

The goal of all relationships should be mutual suicide instead of marriage

This is the second time I've seen someone get carried out of Applebees on a stretcher before noon

May

Waiting for the cocaine fairy to burst through my bedroom window and make my life better for an hour then much worse for ~72 hours

I have learned to not only distrust, but also vaguely resent the initial burst of hopefulness immediately following my first cup of coffee

Is there any way for me to earn money by making people's lives a little bit worse with my grating personality?

On the subway with a person who I am ~70% sure is my roommate but we keep making eye contact and neither of us are saying anything

A homeless guy with rainbow cornrows got on the subway and said 'I'm an alien from outer space' then played extremely loud saxophone until 3 children cried

Apparently I woke up in the middle of the night crying and shouting and whimpering but all I remember is a dream where I had sex with a goat

'Fast and Furious 6' ? More like 'I hope i die in my sleep tonight', am I right you guys?

June

If I had $1 for every time someone has apologized immediately after ejaculating on me I'd have 1 more dollar than I would have had 5 minutes ago

I would do some seriously degrading shit for a Macarthur grant

Imagine a pregnancy test that immediately explodes and kills you when it turns out positive

So do you guys still like art? I only like basketball now

Eating a styrofoam cup full of ice cream while watching 'Japanese Woman is Molested in a Train: Part 2'

Cashier at Duane Reade wrapped my box of tampons in 3 bags then put it in another bag then said 'Is this bag big enough?'

Tao is forcing people to smell his shirt in line for the Guggenheim

Imagine Werner Herzog struggling to ram his dick into a cold block of cheddar cheese

July

'Getting fetal' should be a thing people say referring to fetal position. Like 'I can't wait to go home and get fetal after work today'.

Inside my cubicle, nobody can hear me scream

Sweat is useful in cooling you down and disguising your tears

Suicide #lifehack

The cops let me keep my cocaine and fireworks. God bless america

The only way to maintain relationships, I've learned, is to lie to constantly and expect nothing and act in ways that are unpredictable and insane

People only have sex with me to prove that they are as depressed as they say they are

'Living' is just the longest and most painful form of suicide

Was gonna tweet 'I accidentally got cornstarch in my bangs' but what I really mean is 'I was experimenting with putting cornstarch in my bangs'

Don't ask me about my hair (I put cornstarch in it)

You only don't live past 30 once

'No old friends either' -Drake

A grocery store employee didn't know what Pop Tarts were so he directed me to another employee who also didn't know what Pop Tarts were

All this cocaine is going straight to my uterus

August

I told my roommate we should keep the mouse because there's a pretty big chance its actually a very tiny dog

I want my funeral to be a pizza party with 500 pizzas and nobody is allowed to leave until all the pizzas are eaten

Watching someone do pushups while I lay on my stomach in a bed and eat a ~300 calorie piece of cookie

Hello xanax my old friend

I'm the only person at da club with a yeast infection

Gonna put 'depressed and selfish' under the special skills section in my resume

September
'I'll just google the dosage' -famous last words

I'm AT LEAST an alcoholic

Contrary to popular belief, drugs are, in fact, 'the answer'

Eating banana flavored klonopin and quietly rubbing myself on things

I just vomited at a place called 'Hot and Crusty'

Green eggs and help me

Every day I'm sufferin'

Just whipped out my bag of kiwis on the subway platform and everyone was like 'Damn, check out THAT girl'

If you don't know how to be happy and you know it clap your hands

October

I will look back at this period of my life and think [abandoning this tweet, too grim]

'Too stupid to lie' is now a characteristic that I find sexually attractive

I did it all for the... (don't remember)

An extremely smelly homeless guy stumbled out of a liquor store then got really close to my face and said 'Hi, I'm the real Slim Shady'

I met a fun guy at the bus stop who likes my giant bottle of wine (I found some klonopin on my floor just now and ate it) #funguy

I'm looking to get carried out of Applebees on a stretcher tonight

What if shittier books were more flammable

I'm excited to have more time to play World of Warcraft and do cocaine alone in my room now that nobody is having sex with me

Had a dream that Parker Posey said to me 'Theres a bank that doesn't have ATMs but business is booming because they sell turkeys for super cheap'

I'm high on cocaine and eating a burrito on a stoop in front of Planned Parenthood at 4:30pm on a Thursday

They're playing 'Ignition Remix' at Planned Parenthood

I wanna star in a porn movie called 'One Girl, One Macbook' (the porn involves me putting an entire Macbook in my vagina, I think)

Hating myself is my main bitch and hating other people is my side bitch

November

Relationships are like smoking crack. The extremely euphoric high, then the comedown and the horrible, inevitable, insatiable fiending

I don't actually enjoy parties or relationships, I just like the idea that I could maybe be in either of those things

Vague relationships where neither person wants to feel comfortable or happy, thats that shit I used to like

My milkshake makes all the boys run away to Mexico... ?*

---

* Tweeted this when my boyfriend flew from our home in New York to Mexico immediately after I tried to break up with him. Another boyfriend had done the exact same thing 2 months prior.

Today my editor said if he had a threesome with me he wouldn't be able to get it up and I said 'Every threesome I've had ended in tragedy'

All the drugs are broken

Self help book titled 'How To Hate Other People More Than You Hate Yourself'

An advertising campaign for the McRib says that it has no bones, which means there is more pork, which means there is 'more sandwich'... ?

I never clear my browser history after watching porn but I'm really nervous about people hearing me pee

If the only things that make you feel happy are things that make you feel much worse in the long term and you know it clap your hands

The main effect of all drugs is wanting more drugs

Spent Thanksgiving on a plane eating crackers so high on xanax that I thought a poetry reading was happening in the aisle

December

Today I ate 2 birth control pills because I like pills and I have no self-control

'Life Is An Unbearable Nightmare No matter How Much Raw Vegan Food You Eat' would be a pretty name for a girl

Extremely stoned and incredibly stoned

I have PTSD from being an active participant in my own life

The McRib really stresses me out

All I want for Christmas is infinite money and the ability to reproduce asexually

The Unbearable Unavoidable-ness of Being

Ball so hard I somehow peed on everything but the toilet

Yeah I'll fuck my cat, I'll fuck all your cats

If I eat a child will I become pregnant with the child

I stand with the 50% of people in Iceland who don't deny the existence of elves

Why does 2013 get to stop being a year but I have to continue being Mira

2014

January

My cat rose from my pile of dirty laundry like a phoenix rising from the ashes

Check it out people: the drugs probably aren't making you insane, you're just like that

Is Drake happy?

Cormac McCarthy's ex-wife pulled a silver handgun out of her vagina, then pointed it at her boyfriend during a heated argument about aliens

Cormac McCarthy's ex-wife said 'Who is more crazy, you or me?' to her boyfriend while fucking a silver handgun... my girl

All I want in life is a medium rare steak and a silver handgun to put in my vagina

I have a flamethrower in my vagina

Pulitzer prizes should be given to whoever can fit the most items in their vagina

Sometimes I go through the twitter feeds of people who I feel have 'wronged me' and read all their tweets in a high-pitched sarcastic tone

The scariest people in the world are people who want to constantly tell you how happy they are. Second scariest people are serial killers

What I'm looking for right now is a boyfriend who doesn't talk ever and won't have sex with me even when I ask him to

'Are any of us ever going to make money?' she shouted into the endless void

My other twitter account is a fulfilling life

Kim Kardashian's hair blows the wrong way in the 'Bound 2' music video

I'm bringing basic back

I'm not a man-baby. I'm a man, baby

Despite all my rage I am still extremely passive all the time

I would be interested in an MFA program that teaches you how to forget about poetry entirely and learn how to do something that's actually useful

I guess I started writing poetry because I want to be a famous billionaire

If you don't support my raging alcoholism, then I don't support your artistic ventures. Thats life

Rap game make the same mistakes repeatedly until you die

Why won't anybody stop me from doing me?

I like my men how i like my disco: dead

February

I don't think people actually enjoy kissing, they just do it, like how people eat potato skins in mashed potatoes sometimes

It's called body dysmorphic disorder, get into it bro

Is being a baby really awesome, or like constant torture?

I feel too overwhelmed by the idea of doing things to be able to actually do things

So many twitter followers, so little cold hard cash

I'm honing my lesbianism

My vagina needs to start wearing tiny versions of all the clothes I wear on my body

What if we already died and this is some other thing and it doesn't stop

I'm up all night to get grumpy

I'm cold and poor and upset

Fuck me once shame on you, fuck me twice shame on you

I feel huge and sassy

I'd fully rather be unhappy than assert myself in any way

So you like your dog? You'll like it even more when it's dead and in my vagina

My new thing is going to important literary events dressed like a homeless maniac

People are starting to look more like Fred Durst lately

Sex drugs and Understanding

Reality TV show called 'So You Think You Can Fit This Toaster In Your Vagina?'

Just because I'm addicted to alcohol doesn't mean I'm an alcoholic

Saw a naked toddler running free through LAX airport

we've been waiting 8 hours for weed #awp14[*]

March

Drugs have made me ~20% more lesbian than I was last month

I haven't slept in ~48 hours but I can't fall asleep now because I'm too busy smoking weed and doing drastic things to my hair

---

[*] AWP stands for Association of Writers & Writing Programs. It is an annual writer's conference. I went in 2014. The conference was being held in Seattle. The first day I got there I spent 8 hours sitting in a house waiting for weed to be delivered. The weed was delivered at 9pm. When it was delivered we smoked it in the hot tub, then fell asleep. We never went to the conference.

I recently witnessed someone, upon realizing he had lost an argument, say 'I'm right' and walk away. Very advanced technique.

My face is so big I bought it at Costco

Feels cruel when people are like 'you're so young, you have so much life ahead of you'

The main goal of every drinking game is to drink until you die

'Dying a slow and painful death' is the only possible outcome of everything

I throw my hands up in the air sometimes and people are like 'Mira, stop'

'Bitch Don't Kill My Vibe' is a song about people trying to convince you to stop crying when you're crying for no reason

'Maybe I should have gotten an MFA' -suicide note

I'm ~5% less lesbian now than I was last month

The reason I'm so passive is because my will to live is far lower than average

Reality TV show called 'Figure Out How Many Tampons Are In My Vagina Only By Looking At My Facial Expression'

I'm gonna spend this 3 hour car ride repeatedly hoarding more and more tampons in my vagina

I'm the Lebron James of pissing myself in other people's cars

I got a tampon stuck so far up my vagina this one time. Y'all would have been amazed, it was really up there. It was almost gone for good

'Smoking weed and sleeping' is the new 'making art'

Ima just go grab a bunch of shit and put it in a bucket and tell myself I make art

I'm not wearing a bra to my baby sister's baptism
(I'm a Jew)

Roll up to this baptism looking like a crazy stoned
lizard

Thought the past tense of 'poured' was 'porn'

Nap city bitch nap nap city bitch

My brother said 'What are you doing?' while I was
sprinkling raw cabbage on a slice of pizza and I
said 'making a salad'

A Supposedly Fun Thing I'll Do Until It's Not Fun
Anymore

I'm afraid any baby I have is going to look like the
evil unibrow baby from The Simpsons

April

For April Fools Day I fooled myself into thinking
my life is worth something (April fools!)

Heard what sounded like a fish flopping around in my kitchen while extremely stoned and freaked the fuck out, then I remembered its raining

My milkshake makes all the boys run screaming from my yard

A good metaphor for my personality is unwanted pregnancy

It's not who you think about during masturbation that counts, it's who you aren't ashamed to think about after

I would want to fuck Drake if I were in a good place emotionally, but I never am, so...

My next book will be handwritten on a bunch of loose pieces of paper and shoved into a plastic grocery bag thats sealed closed with duct tape

I want Lil Wayne to spit on me in a loving, fatherly way

The secret to productivity is getting drunk within an hour of waking, I've learned

Somewhere out in the ocean dolphins are fucking each other's blow holes and look at you, you're just sitting there

Figuring out how to play Second Life* is more difficult than anything in my first life

I got 99 problems and it is fully in my power to fix all of them but I choose not to

You're only as sad as you feel

Your ambition is fucking it up for the rest of us

When in doubt, write about stuff that makes your parents feel weird and bad

Just had the thought 'What if I don't know Shakespeare's last name?'

My turn ons include: convenience

---

* Second Life is a massive multiplayer online role playing game

Performance art piece where I play the victim my whole life

I have PTSD from losing my phone in my bed one time a few years ago

The party dont start till I hide in my room during the whole party

Quietly binge eating during at a party in my own house

We go together like childhood trauma and adolescent drug habits

It's pancake o'clock, bitches

I like my men how i like my coffee: dead and in my basement

I feel deep shame every time I eat food but I have no qualms about doing cocaine nonstop for a week

Crackheads need rise up and reclaim 4/20

Nobody told me that 'The Notebook' begins with Ryan Gosling getting a girl to go on a date with him by threatening to kill himself

One time my ex-boyfriend let me snort his cocaine at a party, then I told him I had a clove of garlic in my vagina and I could taste the garlic in my mouth

News flash: we're already in hell

A few months ago I decided that I wouldn't have sex with people who call me 'Eeyore' or 'Lil Homie' and I have become a lot happier since then

Covering old food dishes in my room with paper towels like putting a blanket over a dead body

Is that a massive inferiority complex masked by an unsustainable drug habit, or are you just happy to see me?

I'm crying and eating cold potatoes alone in my car wearing a sweater covered in baby vomit like the sexy, dateable woman that I am

When I'm on my period nobody else is allowed to be on their period. Do you hear me?

I will go to my grave claiming to be able to write while stoned despite knowing for a fact that is 100% not true

I am familiar and comfortable with James Franco's brand of 'smarmy bro'

We go together like an active social media presence and deep-seated emotional problems

I'll fuck the face of every dad in north America

I'd rather tell people I'm a junkie and a prostitute than say I'm working on a novel

I'm amazed at my own ability to be crazy for an extended period of time

If you wanna be my lover, you gotta seriously re-evaluate your life choices

Imagined hiring like 25 interns and then it turning into a 'Lord of the Flies' situation

'Eating out of boredom instead of hunger' is the new 'writing a novel'

Face so big you can see it from the back

Drop it like it's your last shred of dignity

Dostoyevsky? More like
Dotstoyvvseykystoveffvskffskyfffff

I'm gonna fire my intern if he doesn't fix my life-long emotional problems and body image issues

May

I like the part in airports where cops touch me

Open letter to the person asleep next to me: are you really asleep and can we eat chicken wings for breakfast

If you can't handle me at my unsustainable drug habit, then you dont deserve me at my eating disorder

Catch me dipping solid butter in liquid butter

Excited to eat cheese and watch Spongebob for the next ~5 hours

I'm the Jonathan Franzen of bleeding through my pants in social situations

What if it was normal to have a kitchen in every room of the house

June

My ability to binge eat while high on Adderall brings all the boys to my yard

Sang 'gotta whole lotta limes' to the tune of 'Whole Lotta Love' stoned and alone and holding limes in my kitchen

The road to emotional stability is paved with weight gain

I do not want to be involved in any 'journey of self-discovery' ever again, is that understood?

I would watch a reality TV show where people on Xanax try to navigate their way out of a corn maze

I was looking for some cake and then I found a cake... and heaven knows I'm miserable now

Gonna get stoned and braid my hair like Coolio, stay tuned[*]

I'm bringing clingy back

Sorry, I'd love to hang out with you but this alcohol isn't going to drink itself into incoherence and liver failure

Theres like 10 Chinese men in my dads house and I don't know why. He's speaking to them in Chinese. I didn't know my dad knew Chinese

Constantly doing a bunch of different drugs so I never become dependent on one specific drug is my anti-drug

One big room, full of sad bitches

---

[*] Coolio retweeted this.

Sad bitch contest, I'm in first place

Being narcoleptic seems dope

My plan is to surround myself with people who will become successful, so when they have a child I can babysit for a fraction of their income

Here comes the part where I eat chips

My cat keeps running away every time I try to shed my uterine lining onto her

I have so many devices to look at the same ~5 websites

If you can't handle me at my unsustainable drug habit, then you don't deserve me at my sober but equally as insane

Dreamt I had to read Infinite Jest in front of a crowd but I could only find the Dave Eggers foreword so instead I made up a story about horses

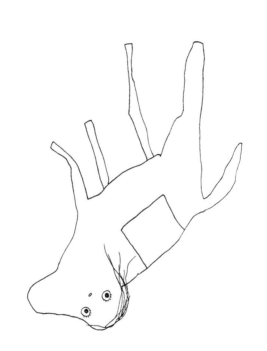

Performance art piece where I spend my early 20s staring at my computer screen alone in my bed-room all day and night

My whole life feels like this one time I offered a friend some potato chips at a party and then he threw the chips everywhere and sobbed

Is it too late for my mom to abort me

'I'm too fat to fit in this car' -me re a normal sized car

For fathers day I got you these lifelong emotional problems

Turn down for the emotional repercussions of fa-ther's day

Please don't stop posting photos of your dads

I like looking at your dads

Whats a good dose of Xanax for a 4 month old?

In an ideal world nobody would make art and everyone would dedicate themselves to playing video games full-time

My activities for the next few months include and are definitely limited to: smoking weed, looking at my cat, not showering

'Horses aren't even human' -a big discovery I thought I made while very stoned

Does Niki Minaj still do her 'extremely crazy' voice, or is she mostly done with that? Anyone have info on this?

You know what i could really use right now? A giant comfy bed and like 14 kittens and 5 human babies and the bed is also a bathtub but nobody drowns

BRB while I make a bunch of sims that look like me and put them in a house with no doors then light the house on fire

Animal Crossing is the only place I feel safe anymore

I wanna watch a TV show thats like, only good guys and they keep succeeding at stuff and nothing bad happens

If I'm not supposed to put all my eggs in one basket, then where the fuck do I put them?

Hey thats pretty cool basket, can I put all my eggs in it?

Everyday I'm sufferin'

I may not be confident or ambitious but at least I'm not confident and ambitious

It's only charming until you realize I'm actually like this

Told someone I couldn't hang out because I'm too stoned to drive, then followed it up with 'but if I get stoned enough I can teleport'

Pulitzer prizes should go to whoever can use their ex's parents' Netflix account for the longest amount of time after the relationship ends

Taking a break from writing for the next couple days to focus on making myself depressed enough to want to write

I haven't eaten in like 30 hours but don't worry because I plan to drink at least 7 margaritas tonight

Mercury in retrograde? More like I'm permanently insane no matter what the fuck Mercury does

July

For 4th of July I'm gonna sit in my driveway and blow shit up by myself. Nobody is invited except all the beers in my fridge

My favorite part of 4th of July is the part where I end up drunk and on fire alone in my driveway

One time on 4th of July my uncle and I tried to burn an American flag but it was plastic and it melted and we both got badly burned

Red white and sad

Last 4th of July I smoked crack and ate a pile of meat with my hands

So excited to quietly vomit on myself at this wedding

Should I make a speech? I know ~4 people here including the bride and groom

Hire me to quietly sit on a couch and tweet at your wedding

There was a time in my life when all parties I went to ended with me eating snacks alone in the host's bed (I don't go to parties anymore)

A blurb I did for a book thats about to be published is ~50% plagiarized from someone's Amazon review of a Jonathan Franzen book

Ambitious people are just trying to get to the part of life where you can stop being ambitious faster than everyone else... right?

'Sorry, I can't hang out today. I have to smoke weed and stare at this tree for a few hours. Then

it's bed time.' -me, every day

I like how when babies get bored with something they just lay on the ground and scream. More people should do that

So excited to eat weed candy and drink beer and stare at my phone at a literary event tonight

Dying young is the only nice thing I can do for my publisher at this point

'It all went downhill the second she mixed weed lemonade with absinth' -my friends and family at my funeral tomorrow

Meet me at the club, it's going down (which is giving me a lot of anxiety and I need a ride home)

Just read on Buzzfeed that depressed people have an 'unusually realistic worldview' (nice)

I can't believe its legal to eat ice cream with whipped cream on top

Can't wait to tell my grandchildren how I spent my early 20's staring at a computer screen and experimenting with starving myself

Shout out to doing 3 sit ups while holding my computer in my hands and calling it 'enough exercise for the rest of the week'

What I lack in skill I make up for in denial

Too google-able to get an office job, not google-able enough to earn a livable salary

When I cry, you cry (just like that)

I look so stoned that I caught a glimpse of myself in the mirror and didn't recognize it as my own face

Why is being alive so expensive?

I'm like 'Are you there God? It's me, Mira' and God is like 'This bitch again?'

I'm crazy (reminder for myself)

People are always like 'lets go to a bar' and I'm like 'okay, but what about the donut store?'

I had this idea to go raw vegan but then I had another idea to eat pizza with bacon on it

Asking me to maintain an office job is like asking a whale to fit into a normal sized condom

That gorilla they taught sign language to is gonna start fucking shit up and attacking people any day now. If i was that gorilla I'd be so pissed.

If you don't prominently display the wifi password in your home or business, is that because you like watching people suffer?

Don't you wish your girlfriend was scared and needy like me?

When I die, bury me with my unpaid intern. I don't care if he is still alive.

I hope the wifi password is prominently displayed in hell

I have some questions: do sloths have sex really slowly and does it take obese people longer to starve to death?

When I say I'm 'working on my manuscript' usually I'm stoned and staring at a plant

Basic as I wanna be

Being an 'artist' means being unbathed, unproductive and alone 99% of the time but saying I'm a 'writer' when attractive people ask me what I do

I plan to die doing what i love: lying down without anyone expecting me to do anything else

I only go to parties so I can ask people if they know of any baby panda videos I might not have seen yet

I'm so impressed by people who can make professional phone calls without taking drugs beforehand

My editor asked me to fax him and I was like

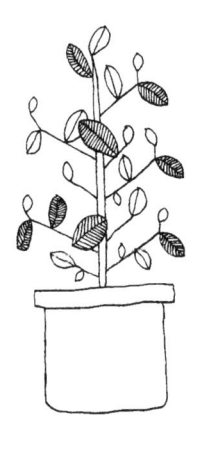

'Okay sure, and after that I will send Abraham Lincoln in a horse drawn carriage to deliver you a dinosaur'

I read that book 'How to Win Friends & Influence People' and it taught me that I prefer to be alienating and uninfluential

If I had a dollar for every eyebrow I have, I would have one dollar

If you're happy and you know it, keep it to yourself

I need a new gynecologist and a new drug dealer. Ideally they would be the same person

My resume just says 'please don't google me' written in my own blood

I'm alone and stoned at the bar at PF Changs in the airport. Theres 4 bros sitting near me who seem like they came here specifically to party. They're doing tequila shots.

Theres an infant on the cover of Time magazine, or I'm way more stoned than I think I am

August

Admitting you have a problem is the first step towards not solving the problem

My favorite part about traveling is the part where I quietly stare at my computer screen indoors

Can't wait to have kids so they can be even more fucked up than I am

Eating and tweeting is the new exercising and having friends

People who regularly go to parties for fun are more mysterious to me than black holes

If you don't get personal satisfaction exclusively from drugs and other people's misfortune I feel bad for you, son

I got 99 problems but a thriving social life ain't one

Shout out to myself for having the personality of

someone with a traumatic childhood even though my childhood wasn't that traumatic

Sleep so hard I wake up exhausted

When I say I'm a 'writer' what I really mean is 'I need like 7 hours per day to fuck around on the internet by myself or I'll go insane'

Leave me alone. Can't you see I'm busy complaining about the natural repercussions of my own actions?

Reality TV show called 'Why Do You Think Anyone Wants To See That Photo Of Your Penis?'

My favorite part about having one life is ruining it with excessive drug use and poor impulse control

My face is so big that children are afraid of me

When I walk down the street children cling to their mothers and point at me and say 'Mommy, how does her face even fit on her head?'

My Saturday night plans include digging a medium sized hole and living in it until I die

Oh, you like exercise and vegetables? That's cool but I prefer candy and dropping out of college

Real friends make plans to hang out then decide to tweet from the safety of their respective beds while openly ignoring each other's texts

Today I angrily shoved a lot of bread in my editor's shoe and screamed at him when he tried to take it out. Publish me

The idea of anyone expecting me to be a 'bad bitch' seems terrifying and stressful

Pick up line: Hey baby, are you my dad? Because I will never be enough for you

Shedding my uterine lining all over everything is one of the many ways I am cultivating my Extremely Glamorous lifestyle

Pick up line: One time I ate a cheeseburger with donuts instead of buns. Now please take a seat

while I describe what the texture was like.

I once dated a guy who thought heroin would cure his alcoholism. I also dated a guy who said his favorite food was 'chicken fries' from Burger King

The very rare and highly underrepresented male perspective

I wish a Jehovah's witness would come to my house. I'm technically Jewish but I'm also really lonely

I like my men how I like my hopes and dreams: dead

I like my men how i like my coffee: having qualities that make me become completely reliant on them and giving me anxiety attacks

Pulitzer prizes should go to whichever author has received the most unsolicited dick pics

What I lack in redeeming qualities I make up for in blaming my dad

At Chipotle in the Dallas airport there is a woman whose only job appears to be screaming 'CHIPOTLE' at people who are already eating Chipotle

My main strategy in social situations is to be obviously the most stoned person there

Good thing I have no idea where my car is, because boy am I too stoned to legally drive it

Dance like nobody is watching, tweet like your parents neglected you as a child

If this new Taylor Swift song doesn't immediately solve my lifelong emotional problems I'm gonna punch my unpaid intern

A cool thing is that stuff can always get worse and it usually does

Don't you wish your girlfriend was an insane burden like me

Gonna ask my unpaid intern to explain to me what the point of a cock ring is

I can't believe people voluntarily to go to music festivals

If you bully a depressed person they will suddenly find the will to live. Kind of like when you yell at a dog and it learns to speak english

I know I'm not adopted because my dad just smoked a ton of weed then took a town car 5 blocks to a Mexican restaurant

Organizing a music festival and not giving free Xanax to all attendees seems inhumane

I can't go out I am busy opening the twitter accounts of people who have wronged me and shouting 'NOBODY CARES ABOUT YOU' at my computer screen

The part I don't understand is why people stop eating when they're not hungry anymore

Don't you wish your girlfriend completely let herself go the minute she realized you probably aren't gonna leave her anytime soon like me?

Skip the honeymoon phase and go directly to the getting fatter phase

Friendly reminder that Wikipedia describes David Bowie's cocaine habit in 1975 as 'astronomic'

Friendly reminder that David Bowie spent all of 1975 in a state of 'psychic terror' and was morbidly afraid of Jimmy Page

Friendly Reminder that in 1975 david bowie told Rolling Stone magazine that his semen was being stolen by witches

My boyfriend's music is playing in my gynecologist's office

I know for a fact some of you people swallow actual semen all the time but still claim to be grossed out by mayonnaise. I see you.

Pick up line: Hey baby, wanna come over and make a character in my Animal Crossing town?

So glad I came to this party so I could get drunk and tweet alone in the bathroom

I'm going to sleep and I'm not waking up until Jonathan Franzen announces that his next book will be 300 photos of his own penis

Dirty talk: 'You like it when i tweet about your personal life? Say it again. Tell me you like having your privacy invaded.'

September

Nuva ring toss

I don't feel bad for anyone who has 99 problems. Thats not very many problems.

I have a fetish for being murdered in my sleep

Alienate Everyone Who Has Ever Cared About You Using This One Weird Trick

'How To Lose a Guy in 10 days' seems like a cheap trick. If you really want to lose a guy you have to slowly break him for multiple years

If you're happy and you know it you're just not thinking

The fat from my tits is migrating to my face

I'm thinking about faking pregnancy for attention

An intervention sounds so fun. It's just everyone you love gathering together specifically to talk about your problems

Don't hate the player, hate their dad

The main purpose of making art is to use 'being an artist' as an excuse to flake on social situations

If they don't have free cocaine and whiskey at this baby shower I'm leaving

My sweatpants are becoming part of me like Venom with Spiderman

Turn down for everything

Why didn't anyone tell me I have to live with myself before I made all those horrible decisions

Here is how babies are made: when a man and a woman love each other very much, the woman eats a nuva ring, which makes her pregnant

0 to uncomfortably stoned real quick

People who do shots of tequila alone at airport bars are the real heroes

Said 'Sorry, I'm on Xanax' after telling the bartender at the airport that I just got my period

Earlier my mom asked me if I'm becoming anorexic and I said 'It's flattering that you think I have self-discipline'

Live slow but die young anyway

As soon as anyone starts using the term 'safe space' I no longer feel safe

Why can't there just be a fun cult where people do drugs and hang out and nobody gets killed or traumatized?

I feel enormous and sassy like a hippopotamus on Adderall

I saw a store in the airport that only sells tiny cupcakes and was moved to tears

I had to take Xanax immediately after seeing the store that only sells tiny cupcakes because it was too exciting and I started panicking

I'm so high and sleep deprived that I saw 3 people sitting behind a counter and assumed none of them had legs and that felt normal to me

I basically got from New York to Los Angeles by sitting in a bunch of different places for 6 hours

I saw the best minds of my generation destroyed by Twitter

Crying in public seems dope

Skip the honeymoon phase, go directly to the giving up on shaving my legs phase

When I say I 'only smoke weed at night' what I mean is that I always smoke weed at night and I only smoke weed during the day most of the time

0 to yeast infection real quick

Boy bands are entire industry dedicated to teen girls objectifying beautiful men. That's so dope

The next iPhone is gonna be the size of a football field and you will have to run long distances to use apps

I'm gonna give up on writing and dedicate myself full time to making tiny hats you can put on your penis

I'm gonna run for office and my political platform will be that we need to legalize caffeinated Four Loko

If you can't handle me at my stoned and staring at a plant then you don't deserve me at my stoned and watching TV

The boy who cried 'friend zone'

Started from the bottom now we still at the bottom

I own like 5 satanic bibles because my dad kept thinking it would be funny to give them to me for Hanukkah

I fuck heavily with man-hating feminism

Hey, I like your basket. Whoa, look at that thing over there! *puts all my eggs in your basket while you're distracted*

What I lack in skill and motivation I make up for in delusions of grandeur

Most people on the internet love expressing their outrage about current events but I just came here for the porn

First name Dick, last name Pic

November

Made a hot date with myself to eat a bunch of

pickles and smoke weed until I suffocate

When someone writes a think piece what they're really trying to say is 'acknowledge that I'm in pain too'

What I lack in money I make up for in body fat

I take every possible opportunity to tell people about my chronic yeast infections but each time I pretend like I'm embarrassed about it

A guy on this plane asked a kid to switch seats with him so he could be next to me, then I said 'I'm too high to talk' and we sat in silence for 6 hours

Roses are red, violets are blue, I am poor and directionless

I plan to die doing what I love: lying down and having no plans for the future

I saw a guy in his car masturbating and eating chips at the same time and I was like 'I see you over there doing you and I respect that'

Ask your doctor if unmasked fury is right for you

My face is stealing all the fat from my ass

My anaconda don't want none unless it's super convenient for me

Being high on drugs seems way safer than being high on life

I like men who look like Squidward but talk like Eeyore

Kim Kardashian's ass is nothing compared to my big round oily face

Congratulations! You aren't pregnant. Now just sit back, relax, and bleed out of your vagina for multiple days

I'm just a soul whose intentions are good, oh lord, please don't let me be out of weed

Which brand of antidepressant will turn my internet addiction into cash

People always wanna go to bars at night and I'm like 'thats cool but when is the part where I eat chips in bed?'

I can't believe people still make art when there is so much porn to watch

December

If you suffered in 2014, you'll suffer in 2015. New year, same life. Merry christmas we're all gonna die

@miraunedited[*]

2012

September

i have no idea what people do on unedited accounts

read 'lamar odom' as 'you're doomed'

i don't feel afraid of dying but i feel really afraid of not dying

all penises are pretty much the same

WHERE THE SAD MEN AT?

cool sex trick: mostly pretend to be dead except say 'good job' sometimes

i've seen media coverage about a fat dachshund on ~4 different news outlets in the last hour. it's 9/11

the girl i'm babysitting pointed at a pile of ketch-up and said 'it's a girl'

this account feels like i'm rolling around in fiber-glass insulation

thought 'im high, im high on painkillers... pain-killers... drugs... i love america... spaghetti'

sometimes i get sweaty when i'm editing tweets. thats why i made this account

sometimes people say 'is your twitter a joke or should i be worried' haha what's up with that you guys follow me on twitter dot com

in the past i have felt aversion towards violently acting out, but it seems fine now

cant stop reading 'rosh hashanah' as 'rosh hahahaha'

emotions that make me sweaty: confusion, panic, anger, embarrassment, excitement, arousal, de-spair, hunger, drunk

i sat next to an attractive guy and he sighed loudly and switched seats

seems like if i took enough different types of drugs, the effects would balance out and i would feel sober. what do y'all think about that?

i am acting out. what do y'all think about that?

this guy is too attractive for me to feel attracted to him but i would like him to punch me in the face sometime

my philosophy professor pointed toward the ground at nothing and said 'look at this thing' and everyone laughed and i said 'i'm that thing'

the dalai lama is ruining my life

i figured out how to smoke hash i think, nobody let me tweet from my main account for the rest of the night

read 'honey crisp apple-almond wafer stack' as 'crispy almond milk honey snack pack apple sausage waffle lemon oprah bars'

i identify with my car because it's shitty and takes up space

if someone compliments my hair and i say 'thank you', i feel like i am accepting a compliment for someone else's hair

i want to be at a party where everyone is crying for different reasons

i smoked weed during my job interview for the medical marijuana dispensary today. it was a nightmare

novel titled 'hahahahahaahahahhaahahahaaaa-hahahahahahahahahahahahahahaahhhahaha-haah wow'

i honestly have no idea what i look like. if i try to imagine my face without looking in a mirror i immediately think of the cookie monster

my dad held up half a hot dog during dinner and said 'this is what my penis looks like'

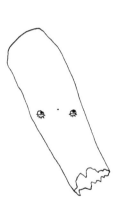

feels like i'm watching everything through tiny eyes that are attached to a tiny face that is attached to my regular eyes

October

touching all the cheese at whole foods

i recommend befriending fucked people because they won't try to make you feel less fucked

let me be shitty in peace

tonight i said to someone 'are you breaking up with me' and he said 'no' and i said 'why not' and then he said 'ok actually yeah'

cried for my entire first day of kindergarten then peed my pants on the second and third day and my mom let me stay home on the fourth day

at a party with a lot of homeless seeming people and the guy i lost my virginity to

party update: i have a yeast infection and a clove of garlic in my vagina

party update: the guy i lost my virginity to is having a baby

party update: i did cocaine in the bathroom with the guy i lost my virginity to. i told him about the garlic in my vagina

party update: trying to get a job being the babysitter for the baby of the guy i lost my virginity to

i went to 2 parties in the last week at the same house and both times i wore the same outfit and did drugs in the bathroom without telling anyone

also the outfit i wore was a shirt without pants and nobody said 'why aren't you wearing pants' at either of the parties

made this account private because i didn't want to alienate people i know in real life but then i remembered were all gonna die and i hate you bitches

currently typing faster and more aggressively than i ever have before in my life, i think

everyday i weigh myself on a scale that says i weigh 200 pounds

fuck nature

almost died while doing jumping jacks in my bathroom

felt aversion to drug addiction while going through an adderall comedown ~30 minutes ago but now drug addiction seems okay/desirable

i'll publish your short story on my ass

who let me make this account

i haven't slept in two days

the parents of the girl i'm babysitting said 'limit her TV time' so i put her in front of the TV and left her there for ~2 hours

i'm afraid to go in public because i don't want people to ask me about my unedited account

the wife of the owner of the place where i get paid to sell weed was a teacher at my middle school

being addicted to crack seems better than not being addicted to crack

I can stand outside comfortably in a dress without a sweater. 0% chance of rain. feel a hurricane is coming soon though...*

update: the smoke alarm went off. my co-worker said 'its just the smoke alarm, not the fire alarm'. i was unaware those are two separate alarms...

update: i have discerned that if there are two separate alarms, it must logically follow that in the event of a fire, both alarms would go off

update: nothing is on fire. hurricane still seems imminent though

update: sweating even though i'm not moving at all

---

* Tweeted from Los Angeles during Hurricane Sandy.

i dont know where i am

might send out a mass email that says 'where am i?'

November

my coworker's two favorite activities are smoking weed and aggressively denying the existence of lesbians

you know when you're on speed, and you can't sleep, because of that... speed... how do y'all feel about this?

JUST WENT OUTSIDE AND IT WAS A FUCK-ING NIGHTMARE

WHATS GOING ON OUTSIDE, IS SOMETHING HAPPENING, THERE WERE SO MANY PEOPLE

ARE THERE NORMALLY THAT MANY PEOPLE OUTSIDE?

how can i lose 10 pounds in the next hour without doing anything

the only way to solve problems caused by amphetamines is to consume more amphetamines

drug addiction would be a 'non issue' if drugs
were free and infinite

if i eat 1 pound of salad and weigh myself immediately, i will be 1 pound heavier. and it's the same if
i eat 1 pound of butter... right?

so then, the idea is that the butter will make me
gain weight later... but the salad won't... ? i don't
understand

also what's up with that thing where you burn
more calories chewing celery than the celery actually has in it?

does that mean that if i only eat celery i will starve
to death without feeling like i'm starving...?

follow up question: what's up with grapes? are
those considered a berry or what?

everybody on the disney channel is selena gomez
except miley cyrus

should i live tweet being at target

i'm at target. smells weird.

this is a nightmare

ok i think i'm done live tweeting now

can anyone recommend me a movie on netflix that is about talking animals but isn't any of the madagascar movies

'fish' can be singular or plural, but 'fishes' is also a word, that makes me feel confused and upset. how do you guys feel about that?

how much xanax are you people gonna take on thanksgiving? trying to gauge what is an appropriate amount

am i mexican? does anyone know

my ass looks like this: ~~*u*~o~~*

OH GOOD THING I STOLE THIS ENTIRE
FUCKING LOAF OF RAISIN BREAD

THANK GOD I HAVE A WHOLE LOAF OF THIS
SHIT

yoko ono designed a $200 jock strap for opening
ceremony

almost finished this entire loaf of raisin bread,
gonna eat salsa with a spoon soon, raisins are
grapes, who wants to fuck

December

red hot chili peppers is odd future... same band

i'm either gonna make coffee or kill myself!

can someone quickly explain the history of the entire world to me?

my favorite math teacher in high school was
named 'bamdad' pronounced 'bomb-dad' (first
name)

bamdad if you're reading this: im a failure now

brett easton hellish

i want to get married so i can get divorced

i didnt exist for so long and now this. what did i do to deserve this?

grandma said about her best friend 'if she came to my house i would have to kill her'

i swallowed an ambien and ~$20 worth of vodka drinks at malibu al's beach bar in the airport

2013

January

is anyone awake, i'm watching dora the explorer, i'm in hell*

---

* The previous night I had taken a lot of MDMA at a New Years eve party, then got in a fight with my boyfriend, at which point we both made out with other people and I ended up sleeping at my uncle's house instead of at his apartment, which I had been living in since moving to New York a few days prior. This was tweeted during my MDMA hangover the next day.

do i have anything i need to apologize for from the past 24 hrs

don't answer that question

feel unable to comprehend simple english and when i walk it feels like i'm trying to walk through peanut butter

lmao if you're planning to live until 2014

feel unable to tweet anything besides variations of 'this is a nightmare' and 'i'm in hell'

the only thing that seems objectively bad to me right now is carbs. everything else including murder seems fine

i've literally never exercised

who has crack?

desperately seeking crack

i feel large and powerful

these shorts are white but they say 'pink' on the ass. seems interesting

salad bar employee heard 'kale edamame lemon olive oil' as 'iceberg lettuce corn no dressing'

don't have a pillow in my apt yet. been sleeping on some towels stuffed into a pillow case

unsure if drug binges make me look healthier or drugs make shitty things look good

can't tell the difference between anything and everything else

no longer have any sense of time, it feels like 9am two days ago

there's really no point in having a door buzzer at this office. if someone came here with a bloody chainsaw i would still buzz them in

i've already buzzed in like 3 homeless people today

does anybody even like being happy

how much would i have to paypal someone to push me in a wheely office chair off the empire state building?

who wants to plath at my place tonight?

NOBODY TOLD ME SNOW MAKES THE GROUND SLIPPERY. NOBODY TOLD ME THAT.

snow is a conspiracy

don't know if this is semen or cocaine on my bed sheets

my book is too small and floppy to do cocaine off of

i would make another twitter account to live tweet this cocaine binge if i wasn't already doing cocaine off my macbook

coworkers are panicking in hushed tones, giving each other dirty looks, binge eating kettle corn, im sitting on the floor next to my desk

if anyone at work asks me to do anything i'm gonna punch the intern

if i ever make a third twitter account call suicide watch

a person just texted me a photo of like a chicken's vagina or something, dead chicken, things are looking up for mira

being severely allergic to things seems sweet (via potential for 'instant death')

if i just keep tweeting then each individual tweet will be less valuable. that is what it's like to be human also

February

beyonce ruined the superbowl with her powerful ass*

---

* Tweeted when the Super Bowl halftime show blacked out during Beyonce's performance.

just ate a huge piece of paper towel, is that okay?

roommate came into the kitchen and saw me making pasta and said 'are you okay' then 'your avocado is ripe, i checked it last night'

i have two bottles of trader joes wine and like 4 tortillas so i don't have to buy any food for at least a month, right?

should i watch full volume porn in dunkin donuts tomorrow and see how long it takes for them to kick me out?

what's up with this whole 'will to live' thing? y'all have that shit?

woke up with an entire uneaten pie in my bed

the protagonist of this food network show is a morbidly obese guy who has eaten a 3 pound, 2,000 calorie omelette every day for the last 6 years

a cool way to express feelings/desires to people

is to ramble nonstop until the person gets over-whelmed and stops paying attention to you

my editor said to me 'taking life advice from you is like taking life advice from a murderous insane retarded bear'

should i start a kickstarter to fund my drug habit

my fridge feels like a physical manifestation of my failure as a person

'is twilight on netflix' -suicide note

i'm about to go to town on a crack rock

'i'm crackin up!' -me after smoking crack

do threesomes make girls more prone to having their periods synced up?

props to the stranger who emailed me about his rash

my boss said 'did you read that email i sent you?'
and i said 'yes' and she said 'so what do you think?'
and i said 'i didn't read the email'

March

people like tweets that are a bunch of unrelated sentences strung together manically without
punctuation

i should just drink mouthwash, right? what am i
trying to prove

i plan to leave this bowl of pasta in my crotch for
another ~2 hours, eat none of it, leave it on my
bedroom floor overnight

ate most of the bread i bought during the ~2 minute walk from the grocery store to my apartment

i don't know how many roommates i have or what
their names are or what they look like

what's the most tactful way for me to ask the intern to go buy a bag of coke then watch me snort
all of it in the bathroom without sharing?

can other people also do an insane twitter thing tonight? i feel like it's always just me doing an insane twitter thing

got beer all over my bed and wall and everything else while trying to shotgun a beer alone in my room

cleaned up spattered beer using my only towel

used 'eco friendly no forks or napkins' option on seamless, but now its like, i have to be responsible for this metal fork...

eating things in bed alone in the dark, wearing 3 shirts and a hat, feeling frustrated about things that haven't happened yet, this is saturday night

i wish i had no boobs and a different face and 4 million dollars

said 'heads we buy crack, tails we don't buy crack' then the coin landed on tails like ~5 times. god is fucking me

they're having another office party... i'm drinking

beer alone... there are 20 pizzas on my desk... all the fish are dead...

everything i'm experiencing lately feels like being aggressively face fucked with a fire extinguisher

i have begun to think of 'consciousness' as 'that shitty thing between sleeping'

interested in getting into an explosive argument with someone in the near future

made a rule that i have to stop drinking coffee by 5pm while planning to buy as many amphetamines as i can afford later tonight

ate ravioli for breakfast, about to eat ravioli for dinner, i'm really 'banking' on an imminent apocalypse you guys

this coffee maker is a cold metal death trap

a funny thing to do while giving a blow job would be quietly die

so what do you guys like more, ice cream or cocaine?

you have a pet goldfish? i'm gonna fuck it

paypal me $900 and ill chop my left tit off with a cleaver and post it to vimeo

April

should i become a hoarder?

here's a thing depressed people like doing: things that make them more depressed

these interns are the bane of my existence

the interns are running wild, the interns have lost their minds, i no longer have control over the interns

should i sell tao 20 fake adderall pills then run away to mexico?

when people tell me they won't strangle me until i'm unconscious what i hear is 'i know what you want more than you know what you want'

the idea of being hit by a train seems like, sexually arousing to me right now

spring has weeded out the 'permanently miserable' from the 'seasonally miserable'

i was having a 'serious relationship conversation' on xanax then this bro was like 'i'm gonna lie this way now' then turned away from me and now he's asleep

every time i think about exercise i immediately resign to being depressed and fat for the rest of my life

i'm gonna be that over eager idiot who commits suicide at the first sign of a zombie outbreak and it ends up being no worse than swine flu

phew i am exhausted from all this sudden useless despair, haha!

earlier i saw a homeless guy masturbating on the train. he was being really quiet and considerate though. i miss him

yo everybody watch out i'm about to come through with some real talk: what's the difference between 'icing' and 'frosting'?

yeah i want a giant fucking platter of meat and a massive jar full of beer, are you fucking me? if you do that will you also strangle me?

haha boy do i love just fucking laying here

should i live tweet an inevitable hellish conversation i'm gonna have in the next 12 hours

May

i can't tell if it would be easier to call my dad and tell him i need my wisdom teeth removed or quietly develop an addiction to painkillers

i can already tell that the worst part about getting mouth surgery is talking to my dad on the phone about getting mouth surgery

saw a child make a quick escape from his stroller and run free before pausing in front of me then crying out of confusion/horror

trying to think of a way to 'retaliate' against [my boyfriend] but that feels a lot like punching a retarded person in the back of the head

this bro is showering and he thinks i'm asleep but i'm not. should i use this opportunity to fuck up his apartment then bounce?

my cab driver invited me over for veal cutlets with him and his wife

why does a cheeseburger get a different name than a hamburger... its the same sandwich...

if all i ate today was 4 garlic knots, then i mysteriously vomited, does that mean i ate nothing? follow up question: can i eat more garlic knots now?

all romantic relationships are a competition to see which of us can make my life more hellish and i always win

should i live tweet doing cocaine on a tuesday? my mom follows this account

what i'm experiencing in life is like one of those roller coasters that just goes straight down really fast with no loops or anything

a cheeseburger walks into a bar and the bartender is like 'sorry, we don't serve food here' (follow me on twitter dot com)

i'm gonna fuck my lamp

this guy on the train has two babies. i feel he is 'hoarding' babies and should give me one

my boyfriend said smoking crack while pregnant is fine and the only problem is the baby is born addicted to crack but the baby gets over it

keep thinking how excited i am to go home and have some 'me time' but then i remembered i am driven insane by my own company

WHY ISN'T MY CRACK DEALER PICKING UP THE PHONE ITS MY BIRTHDAY

seems comforting that i will always be capable of treating myself worse than anyone else treats me

June

i tweet from this account when im worried about things that i wont just talk about directly (via extreme passivity and desire to not seem 'crazy')

i would rather commit suicide than not eat this free(?) pizza i found

someone at my work just like, dramatically took his pants off to reveal spandex bicycle shorts

this guy just told me he's gonna bring a backpack full of quinoa to jury duty

its significantly easier for me to buy crack cocaine than to prove to the government i live in new york

so how many pregnancy tests have you guys taken this week?

would be funny if you could get pregnant from fucking a pregnancy test

lebron james impregnating bitches through the TV screen

i'm literally vomiting pure despair

meekly took 2 slices of free pizza without saying anything to my co-workers then walked back to my cubicle & cried

would describe the way i'm eating sushi right now as 'hoarding sushi in my face'

god i have made so many horrendously poor decisions in my life

yeah mira, go ahead and dip your deep fried sushi in soy sauce. because you know what your oily mayonnaise-soaked carbs really need? salt.

i need an intern who can find me good porn

July

i dropped a soda and it exploded everywhere so i blamed it on the intern

joseph gordon levitt looks like a horrible shitty hot dog

i am ready to sit back and watch myself fuck my life up

i was having a 'hushed' conversation with my co-worker then an ~80 year old man who i've never seen before walked up to us and shouted 'WHERE'S THE PARTY'

i'm having gin and candy for dinner tonight

rap song titled 'everyday i'm late to my internship' to the tune of 'everyday i'm hustlin'

everybody at this paul mccarthy exhibit is afraid to laugh at an hour long video of a guy struggling to maintain an erection so he can fuck a wax doll

i identify with kirby (pink, round, avoids conflict by meekly floating away, eats everything)

you're only as depressed as you feel

any things with cool textures that i could lick tonight?

all roads lead to i hate myself

catch me on my death bed, groping my own ass

i don't want sex, just a meek groping

i cant believe i have sex with men sometimes. what a dumb fucking idea

want to accuse someone of putting a roofie in my drink even though i specifically remember taking drugs voluntarily

iceberg lettuce and crack smell like, really similar

this pillow doesn't belong to me but boy am i drooling on it!

what if i only ate fried chicken today and nothing else (thats what i'm doing)

might drink more coffee, might look at porn on my phone in my cubicle

might eat a burrito now and a burrito for lunch

eat 5 corn chips and a lot of edamame for dinner, cry yourself to sleep, wake up a new woman

oh so now i gotta be the only one tweeting like this?

i've cried more in the last 24 hours than in my entire infancy

i think i just got away with saying the sentence 'i'll shower when this beer'

everyone i've ever had sex with hates me lol

should i make @mira_starving to live tweet my experiment with anorexia?

thoughts of suicide temporarily interrupted by thoughts of the attractive young intern i'm gonna abuse at work later

told the intern he was getting fired and he believed me, it's his first day lol

became aware that the only reason i'm not eating the ice cream in my freezer is because i'm saving it for breakfast

god why is it so hard to google how cocaine affects your menstrual cycle

thought 'a wild table has appeared' after seeing that my roommate had put a table in my room while i was gone

August

i'm like, so much worse than my twitter makes me seem, lol

we should all feel personally responsible for tao today, i think*

spent a few seconds literally screaming in agony and i could do it more but i was told to stop

---

* Tweeted the morning after Tao took mushrooms and threw his computer into a construction site.

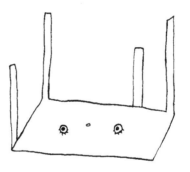

people talk about like, closing your eyes during sex, how that means the sex is bad or something, but i think i always do that, like to concentrate

i recommend trusting nobody because trust = expectation = disappointment. i also recommend destroying your body with drugs and being unhappy

any parties with heroin and beds?

thought a full grown man in the grocery store was a mouse

they don't let you order burgers medium rare at applebees, lol

can everyone stop dicking around and admit that pop tarts are cookies?

im having a hard time formulating a joke about 'softening the blow' by eating before doing cocaine (eating before cocaine, in my experience, makes hangover less bad. blow=cocaine. do u understand?)

obama probably likes fucking, not 'making love', thats why he's president

i ate 2 eggs and some sour candy for breakfast

ate avocados and cookies for breakfast at ~3pm again

this beautiful young intern seems to enjoy being abused by me and also he smells good

more like.... 50 shades of cray....

am i getting a despair induced yeast infection? stay tuned

during dinner my dad said 'is he gonna impregnate you soon?' and 'you don't eat enough' and 'do LSD instead of cocaine' and 'what's wrong with your hair?'

people in my family keep asking 'which one is the active loaf?' meaning 'which of the 3 bread loaves on the table is currently being eaten?'

little do they know all 3 loaves are 'active loaves'

extremely stoned and incredibly afraid

all the cocaine is broken

September

periods are the only thing i can think of where its a problem if you don't bleed

just realized that living in my own apartment means i can buy cinnamon toast crunch if i want to. my name is on the lease, bitches

my uterus wants cheese steak

i'm kind of repulsive, i feel

what are some extremely degrading things i could make tao do for me in exchange for these adderall crumbs i found in my wallet?

what if instead of 'chingy' that guy named himself 'clingy'

every day everyone has to wake up and do things and those things everyone does are supposed to be 'good enough' to continue wanting to be alive… (?)

everything is just a thing to endure… another thing… endless things to endure

if you hate yourself more than anyone else can ever hate you then you're pretty much invincible

would be cool if there was a way to like… relieve yourself of being alive without going through the hassle of committing suicide

things that are difficult for me: maintaining relationships with people i'm not having sex with, showering, team sports

i'm learning how to comfort myself. after that i'm gonna learn how to stop eating and get all my nutrients from the sun via photosynthesis

does anyone know how to turn depression into the kind of anger that motivates me to exercise

my hair is so dirty it's a completely different texture

MY BOSS HAS TWENTY ONE THOUSAND (21,000) UNREAD EMAILS

a benzo a day keeps the void away

mamas gonna black out tonight!

whoever said you can't solve your problems with drugs and alcohol is wrong wrong wrong! :)

i've eaten something like ~15 melty fruit flavored xanax tablets in the past 24 hours

i don't know what my job is so i'm just here eating xanax candies and checking twitter

feel like the token high person at every social event

this morning at 6am someone pulled my blanket off me and said 'do you think there is a game stop near here? i need to buy grand theft auto 5'

walked into work and announced 'i'm high on drugs' and everyone laughed but like....

look at all these nyu freshman who also think their sadness is unique and interesting

tonight at a reading i announced 'i will trade someone 2 of my books for literally any drug' then ended up giving both books away for free

my boss is going through every email she has ever received from linkedin and deleting all 200 of them because she thinks they're spying on her

i feel like this intern goes home to his girlfriend every night and is like 'that sad receptionist at my work is only getting sadder'

i like my drug dealers how i like my men: honest and reliable (just kidding)

straddling that fine line between binge eating and starvation

i'd probably be a pretty good prostitute and a pretty mediocre drug dealer and a terrible star-bucks employee

mama is 'going off the deep end' you guys (referring to myself as 'mama' in this tweet)

tonights the night (for semi-unwanted pregnancy)

these pregnancy tweets are just to make sure that some people i wanna have sex with will avoid having sex with me in the future

today i blew 0.0 on a breathalyzer test and then i fell asleep at the bar

i went to applebees and now i'm at popeye's

October

i'm going to outer space, bitches

'i'm too caffeinated, i just need to straighten myself out' -excuse i used to eat xanax at 9 this morning

i just got invited to play farmville 2 on facebook so things are actually looking up for me

what if i named my first child 'meat cleaver'

how many more hours are left... in... my life...

gonna send my boss an email that says 'dear boss, i'm dead, please don't stop paying me, i love you, all the best, mira'

announcer just said 'the next manhattan bound L train will arrive in like... 15 minutes?' as the train was approaching the station

i think i maybe turned my brother into a drug addict... with my mind....

got my ass grabbed in the liquor store. it was nice to be touched and feel close to someone

i like the part in airports where we get to take our shoes off

what the fuck do you mean the airport bar isn't open at 8:30am

this cop just asked if he can get free refills on his milkshake

PRO TIP: IF YOU'RE SAD AND ALONE IN THE PLACE YOU LIVE THEN YOU GO TO ANOTHER PLACE YOU WILL STILL BE SAD AND ALONE WHEN YOU COME BACK

any sperm donors (i don't trust dads)

i hate all of you almost as much as i hate all of me!

what happens if i stop tweeting, something really bad right

i'm 'inhaling' a burrito on a stoop outside planned parenthood while they decide whether or not i'm poor enough to get free birth control

i spent an hour in a supermarket and i left 5 min ago and don't remember what i bought

at planned parenthood they asked me how many sexual partners i've had and i said 'i don't know off the top of my head' and she said 'oh honey'

at planned parenthood the nurse asked me when i lost my virginity and i told her and she immediately said 'wow did you have boobs back then'

they took my blood pressure at planned parenthood while i was high on cocaine and the nurse said 'it's a little low'

i like winter in new york because it makes everyone look miserable and shitty instead of just me

government funded programs to convince kids that art is bad

war on art

separation of art and state

i'm confident that my identity is shitty enough that nobody will steal it

feels so difficult to be in a relationship or not be in a relationship but some people are in relationships all the time or never... ?

November

just became so overwhelmed with potential food options that i actually cried

the problem with daylight savings is now the appropriate time to get drunk is further away....

what's up with being so depressed you wanna sleep all day then not being able to sleep at night, pretty silly huh

the unseemly and horrifying state of my bedroom is only one of the many ways by which i repel all sexual encounters

i want to organize a suicide bombing but bombs seem surprisingly hard to purchase

i'm nothing if not extremely unreliable

i don't know when i became an angry drunk but it was sometime between last night and this morning

@mira_crying*

* This was an account that my boyfriend made towards the end of our relationship, during a period of time when I was crying a lot. The original purpose of the account was for him to tweet about me crying. He gave up on that immediately after making the account and gave me the password so I could tweet about myself crying instead. I made the account private and began tweeting things that, I felt, were too bleak and unseemly for me to tweet from my public accounts. The sorts of things I didn't want my friends and family to see. This is the first time I have shared it with anyone, though I suspect my (ex-)boyfriend may have been secretly logging in and reading the tweets.

2013

July

Last night I cried for no reason and I did the same thing the night before then this morning I had sex and then I cried again

I didn't tweet while crying last night because I was too busy crying

It would be cool if instead of sleeping people just died... ? (didn't think this tweet through)

I didn't cry during a movie about genocide

August

I'm high on bacon and self loathing and medical grade heroin

I haven't cried for a few days now. About to buy cocaine in daylight

Told my drug dealer this batch of coke isn't as good as the last one and he sounded like he was about to cry

Rendered incoherent by depression

I'm wearing a thong and it feels bleak

This cream thats supposed to make my yeast infection less itchy is making my yeast infection more itchy

I think I've had sex with more people than my mom has

Felt nostalgic for smoking crack while smoking weed

The face I make when I cry brings all the boys to the yard ('all' is an exaggeration but some boys do like having sex with me while I'm crying)

[My boyfriend] turned to me in the middle of snorting a line of cocaine and said 'this shit tastes like yogurt, bro'

September

Today my dad called me 'bitch ass' ~5x then hung up on me and cancelled my credit card

Should I offer the intern some of this mystery powder Tao gave me (it's either ketamine or heroin)

Should I ask someone about heroin/ketamine dosage before I snort this mystery powder or should I just 'wing it'?

So thats what heroin(?) tastes like

Interesting feeling, in my head, the heroin. It's definitely heroin.

I recommend heroin

Heroin made my crotch itchy

Some things I enjoy are: bacon, rebound sex, and heroin

What's a good excuse for having a black eye besides 'I'm experimenting with violent sex because I'm depressed'?

Guess how many people have said 'you look afraid' while listing things they enjoy about having sex with me

My co-worker asked if it was ok for her to bring cocaine and a knife to my stepdad's concert

Two people who have had sex with me in the last week told me they don't want me to lose weight then one of them admitted he was lying

The person who gave me this black eye during sex just tried to blame it on another person who I haven't had sex with in over a week, lol

Like somehow a whole week passed and the black eye just magically appeared now and was completely unrelated to him hitting my face yesterday

I was so close to losing a tampon inside of me last night but I found it. Don't worry everybody it's out now

It's incredible how lost that tampon got last night, I truly could not find it, I didn't know that could happen, it was unbelievable

October

Life is dope and beautiful

You know that Waka Flocka Flame song thats like 'I got my main bitch, and my mistress' ? Well in my experience it's not usually that clear who is the main bitch and who is the mistress.

Oh fuck, does that mean I'm the mistress?

I need a main bitch and a side bitch and they need to have VERY clearly defined roles

I'll mark my main bitch with a name tag that says 'main bitch' and my side bitch with a name tag that says 'side bitch' so nobody gets confused

Neither my main bitch nor my side bitch is allowed to tag me as 'main bitch' or 'side bitch' though. That is how it works now.

I guess I used to like sex

my bboufriendd is bring ing me a sanandcwich what has YRR BOYFINRED DONE FOR UU LATELY

my booyfreiend doesnt like my life choices but at least he STAYYS QUIET ABT IT

It'd be sweet if dick wasn't... a thing... I hate dick

Seems like all my relationships are bad because I call people 'bro' and want to be hit in the face occasionally

Gonna live tweet a break up, lol

We're playing cards #breakuplivetweet

Oh my god how do I do this lol #breakuplivetweet

'I'm gonna make you feel really bad even though you haven't done anything wrong' -me #breakuplivetweet

FEEL GUILTY NOW #breakuplivetweet

He was very nice about me breaking up with him. He thanked me for being honest then asked if he could still 'dick me down' #breakuplivetweet

I said no, re: 'dicking me down' and he frowned #breakuplivetweet

If you like it then you shouldn't have tried to put a ring on it so quickly #breakuplivetweet

Being alive feels pointless and sad 99% of the time, lol #breakuplivetweet

Still going hard with the #breakuplivetweet 11+ hours post break up #breakuplivetweet

I think my (ex-)boyfriend who I broke up with yesterday who 'doesn't do drugs' is asking me to buy him cocaine so he can use it to garner new bitches

Very advanced bitch garnering technique. Feel proud of him

Keep thinking like, it's important i remember to take my birth control, so I don't get pregnant this weekend when I have sex with... a girl

One ex-boyfriend is big on drunk dialing, the other one isn't big on dialing at all

One of my ex-boyfriends has been asleep for 24 hours and the other one doesn't want to interact with me unless I do drugs with him

I used to orgasm easily, orgasming has never been a problem in my life and now it seems to be the only thing between me and a happy relationship

I took my ex-boyfriend to an Indian restaurant to try to be friends and as soon as we sat down he said 'I hate Indian food' then asked me to explain why I broke up with him

Thinking 'I want to quit my job' repeatedly made it easier for me to achieve orgasm just now

My boyfriend (formerly known as 'my ex-boy-friend') doesn't really like me I don't think... he just likes my boobs and hates being alone

Nurturing my side bitches

This Australian I'm hanging out with.... now I know this sounds crazy but... is he really Australian... is that how they actually sound?

This account is truly unedited in a very embarrassing and disturbing way

Not gonna block ex-boyfriend on this account because it seems funnier for him to just get quietly annoyed by how horrible I am 'deep down'

In other news, I got a comically large amount of period blood on my iPhone

I recommend 'The Mindy Project' and not kissing during sex and combining xanax with only a tiny bit of oxy and drinking at noon

Is my main issue with relationships that I call people 'bro'? Is that why I can't be happy?

Everything seems hilariously misguided lately, like slapstick comedy

November

Listening to Taylor Swift is my main bitch and not doing cocaine anymore is my side bitch

'I recognize this behavior as a kind of thing goth girls with low self-esteem would do in high school' -nail on the head description of me by my ex-boyfriend's new girlfriend

I got ex-boyfriends comin' out the woodwork to judge my life choices

Lets just say there is an extremely flaccid penis touching my leg right now and I can't sleep because of it

Extras

A Depressed Person's Failed Review of *Blue Is The Warmest Color*

March 12, 2013

This past month I have been more depressed than maybe any other time in my life. This is partially, or maybe mostly due to having recently been through the worst ending to a relationship that I have ever experienced. Some days I feel worse than others, but most days leaving bed feels impossible. Sex isn't appealing. Drugs are only appealing insomuch as they make it easier to fall asleep and stay asleep for more hours than I normally would. I have consistently avoided social interaction as much as possible. I have something like 25 unread emails that all require thoughtful responses and I am late for at least 5 deadlines to submit writing to different publications.

I have had sex with 5 different people since the break up, despite feeling mostly uninterested in sex and completely uninterested a committed relationship. I am now experiencing a thing

I used to experience a lot as a teenager, where I have sex with someone then feel like I would pay any amount of money for them to leave my bedroom immediately so I can take Xanax and stare at my ceiling for an hour then sleep for 15 hours and spend the next day alternating between being awake for 1 hour and sleeping for 2 hours.

I basically don't eat anymore unless I'm on drugs or someone is cooking for me. I feel afraid of food and embarrassed when I eat too much of it. I have felt insecure about my weight for as long as I can remember (despite being normal or below average size for a person my height, according to my BMI score) but that isn't why I don't eat when I'm depressed. Hunger is a problem that is easily solved, and it's comforting to be presented with a solvable problem when my entire life feels like an out of control nightmare.

That's not to say that what I am feeling is unique, or even interesting. This specific 'brand' of depression seems universal and common. So common, in fact, that I tend to avoid writing about it as to not seem contrived or irritating. Writing about it makes me feel slightly less depressed though, which is why I am doing it now.

I was solicited to write this essay about 3 weeks

ago. It was originally supposed to be a review of the movie Blue Is the Warmest Color. I highly recommend this movie, but I have never written a movie review in my life and I would have no idea where to begin. The enjoyment of movies (or any artform) seems so based on subjective experience that I wouldn't feel comfortable writing anything besides reasons why I enjoyed the movie, and then I would probably also feel inclined to write reasons why other people might not enjoy the movie. I think anybody who has seen the movie could deduce that information on their own without me having to tell them.

I first came to know about Blue Is the Warmest Color through my ex (the one who I recently broke up with). He was a film student and generally more aware of film stuff than I was. When Blue is the Warmest Color won the Palme d'Or at Cannes Film Festival, he told me about it and we were both thrilled at the idea of Lea Seydoux being French and a lesbian for 3 hours. My ex and I are 'no longer on speaking terms', but he called me, while extremely high on cocaine, the night he saw the movie. He saw it with his new girlfriend and recommended the movie to me a lot. I think the conversation ended in his new girlfriend (a former good friend of mine) getting extremely angry and him calling me back to yell at me about [I don't remember]. The conversation felt confusing and upsetting.

For the following week or two I would receive phone calls from my ex almost every night while he – they – were high on cocaine and probably other drugs (that's not to say drugs are 'bad'. I like cocaine too.) I also received a few essay long texts from his new girlfriend explaining reasons why I am shitty and ugly, amongst other things. I haven't said anything to his new girlfriend since we broke up and I don't plan to. I blocked both of their phone numbers and gmail accounts that week.

A couple weeks later, on Friday night, a person who I had begun dating almost immediately after breaking up with my ex was having a party. He threw parties every Friday and I had been to all of them up to that point.

I had recently been thinking about going to Ohio to visit a friend who I had sex with once while she was visiting New York. I liked having sex with her.

The person I was dating said he would stop dating me if I went to Ohio. So, instead of just telling him that I planned to go to Ohio, and allowing him the dignity of breaking up with me himself, I continued to date him for a few weeks, then broke up with him, then bought a ticket to Ohio. Because

that way I could get everything I wanted and he would get hurt instead of me.

When I broke up with him I told him it was because I wasn't ready for an intensely committed relationship, which is exactly what he seemed to want. That was true to some degree. It didn't seem like a good idea to go immediately from one intensely committed relationship to another one, especially considering how messy my last break-up was. However, in retrospect I think I broke up with him mostly due to depression and sleep deprivation from getting calls from my ex every night, then having to wake up at 6am and go to a job that I hated. Clearly, I maneuvered the situation very poorly.

I was no longer invited to his Friday night parties after that.

So, I decided there were only two possible courses of action for me that Friday night: I would either stay in bed, eat all of my Xanax, watch a shitty TV show on Netflix then fall asleep. Or, I would eat all of my Xanax, go see a 3 hour movie about sad lesbians by myself, then fall asleep. I decided on the latter because I had just run out of episodes of Parks and Recreation to watch.

I took the A train a three stops from my apartment in Brooklyn to IFC theater in Manhattan, where I planned to see a 7:15 showing of Blue Is the Warmest Color. I was going to live tweet it, then write a review of it the next day. To my horror, all the showings that night were sold out. At this point I was already extremely high on Xanax and I had a flask of vodka in my purse, which I had planned to drink during the movie.

I walked away from the theater and wandered aimlessly in circles around Washington Square Park on the verge of tears for half an hour.

I was in possession of one of Tao's Adderalls. I had found it on the stoop outside KGB Bar a few days prior, where my friend Scott McClanahan had his book launch party. It's still a mystery to me why Tao decided to hide his Adderall there, and why he called me hours after the party had ended to retrieve it for him.

Anyways, while I was wondering around the park with watery eyes, Tao emailed me asking if I had his Adderall. He was at Bobst Library at the time, which was nearby. I explained to him that I felt lost and confused upon realizing that the lesbian movie was sold out. He said a 3 hour movie about lesbians sounded hellish but he wanted to come

get his Adderall from me and would also be interested in seeing a movie that was 'like Star Wars or
Lord of the Rings or something' (his words). We
decided to live tweet a 9:30 showing of Gravity.

My ex also invited me to see Gravity a few weeks
prior to this. I wanted to go but felt weird and bad
about it, due to the fact that 1.) I had broken up
with him very recently because he cheated on me
with a close friend, who is now his girlfriend, 2.)
his girlfriend publicly dislikes me, and 3.) he, to
some degree, expressed a desire to have sex with
me, which I also wanted, despite having extremely negative feelings about him. I think he ended
up seeing Gravity with his girlfriend.

Tao and I planned to meet at the theater 15 minutes before the movie. I went to Grassroots Bar
in the East Village and gave my phone to the bartender to charge it. I felt really bleak and it must
have shown on my face because the security guard
at the bar asked me what I wanted to drink, then,
per my request, he bought me a glass of straight
gin. After ordering the drink he said 'It's like
you've never known laughter'. I grinned at him,
drank the gin as fast as I could, then immediately
took the my phone from the bartender and left.

I waited in front of the theater for Tao around

9:15, at which point he texted me 'I think I'm at the wrong theater. I'm running'. Tao arrived at 9:30 exactly holding 2 vegan cookies and a giant empty paper bag. I don't understand why he had the bag and I didn't bother to ask him. In the theater I bought a Diet Coke (because I like how it tastes like poison) and poured vodka in it. Tao and I shared the drink. Tao handed me one of the cookies and said 'this cookie is so big'. I agreed and he took the cookie back.

After Gravity we felt unsatisfied. I was disappointed because Gravity was 'sold' to me as a George Clooney movie. George Clooney sort of floated into the ship from the middle of space at random points during the movie, and stayed there for just long enough to make charming jokes about how handsome he is. His main role seemed to be to tell Sandra Bullock to 'calm the fuck down'.

Tao and I decided to live tweet another movie after that. I suggested we see Ender's Game. I enjoyed reading Ender's Game, but the movie was apparently shitty (I haven't seen it and don't plan to). Tao didn't like that idea and suggested we see 12 Years a Slave instead. I said that live tweeting a completely non humorous movie about slavery was probably a bad idea, but then Tao said something like 'we can just shit talk white people' and it immediately seemed okay (keep in mind I was

very high on Xanax).

The movie was impossible to live tweet. There were a lot of scenes of slaves getting beaten. I think I cried 3 or 4 times.

Okay, now jump forward to 2 weeks later: After many unnecessarily intense emotional conversations, I agreed to date the person who I had broken up with previously, before going to Ohio. He was surprisingly still open to dating me, despite the fact that I left him to have casual sex with a woman. I felt (and still feel) incapable of maintaining a relationship, but I enjoy spending time with him and he is incredibly persistent. He was nothing but nice to me before the breakup, and during the breakup for that matter. He also said some really good things about my pubic hair the first time we had sex (I don't shave my pubic hair). He seemed at least better than my last boyfriend.

I told him I was solicited to do a review for Blue Is the Warmest Color and I might get paid some amount of money for it. He came with me to see it. We both ate 20mg of Oxycontin before the movie (which, for those who don't know, is medical grade heroin).

I was completely entertained for the entire 3

hours. The movie begins with extreme closeups of a girl eating spaghetti and having conversations with her parents and classmates in French. I felt like I could easily and would happily watch 3 hours of her eating and speaking French with no subtitles, which was partially (or maybe entirely) due to the drugs I had taken.

I know a lot of straight girls who watch exclusively lesbian porn. I don't do that. I've tried, I really have, but despite enjoying sex with women in real life, I just can't get into the porn version. The kind of porn I enjoy is, unfortunately, the kind that's made to be enjoyed by males. Stuff with titles like 'Hot Asian School Girl Is Abused On Public Train', for example.

That said, despite enjoying sex with women many times in my life, I have never seriously questioned my sexuality until seeing this movie.

While this boy I was with had his arm around me, I began to feel like maybe I have been doing something wrong this whole time. Maybe all of my relationships are a hellish nightmare because I'm really just attracted to women. I found myself inching away from the person I was with during the sex scenes. Not because I felt uncomfortable, but because I began to feel earnestly unsure about

whether or not I wanted to continue having sex with men.

(Note: I was extremely high on opiates. I no longer feel this way. I had sex with him that night and enjoyed it, which was almost disappointing. It seems that my relationships are all a hellish nightmare for some reason other than 'simply' being a lesbian.)

I cried many times during the movie. I felt extremely emotional. It seemed to portray the beginning and end of a relationship in a way that felt very real and very sad. Or maybe it just hit very close to home for me.

As we walked out of the movie, the person I was with asked how I liked it. I said I liked it very much. I asked him what he thought of it and he told me that during a part where I was full on red-faced sobbing, he was thinking about different things he could do to his back porch. (He decided it would be easier to put bricks on his porch than to put wood on his porch.) He also, apparently, was not all that interested in the lesbian sex scenes, and felt 'grossed out' by the close ups of the girls eating. I was shocked. Even people who told me they didn't like the movie at all said they liked the sex scenes. I spent the next hour trying

to explain reasons why I liked it, thinking maybe he would change his mind, but it didn't work.

There was one scene where the two main characters ate oysters. It seemed symbolic of... well, that scene also felt emotional to me. I don't think the person I was with felt emotional about the scene the way I did, but it did make him crave oysters. The next week, before his Friday night party, he decided to make us a dinner that consisted of oysters, steak, potatoes, salad and pie. That meal was probably the best thing that came out of the whole experience.

I think he broke up with me last night, for seemingly no reason. I have received a lot of apology texts from him today. It seems like he thinks we are still dating and we just got in a bad fight. He was maybe too drunk to remember the part where he said 'I don't want to be your boyfriend anymore'.

I don't plan on continuing to date him but honestly, I probably will. I imagine this cycle will occur many more times in the course of our relationship, and probably in all of my relationships in the future. Luckily I have enough Xanax to kill a small army. I'm ready to face the void.

JULY 4, 2013

I woke up to Peter frantically walking around his apartment gathering ingredients for a smoothie. It was 1pm. He told me he had thrown away the crack pipe in a fit of nervous despair immediately after waking up. Throwing away the crack pipe always seemed like a good idea in the morning, but at night we would realize that we could walk half a block to the nearest bodega and buy the exact same crack pipe again. While pouring the contents of the blender into 2 glasses, Peter expressed feeling worse than he had ever felt from a crack hangover and I expressed similar things.

At around 3pm we decided that we should get out of his apartment before dark. We went to a restaurant in Williamsburg that serves you various types of barbecued meats on big metal trays and beer in jars. We drank 2 beers while waiting in line then got a pitcher of beer with our food. After eating what I would estimate to be a pound of meat each, we went to a bar where they serve

giant margaritas in styrofoam cups. We sat on a curb and drank our margaritas in silence.

That night at a roof party in Greenpoint, I broke a pill of xanax in half, then put half in Peter's mouth and half in my own. After stealing illegal fireworks, 4 beers and a massive American flag, we left the party and walked to the nearest Manhattan bound train.

In the subway station we drank America-themed cans of Budweiser. I had just gotten my second public drinking ticket a few weeks prior to this but I was too drunk and high to care if I got another one, or even remember that drinking beers in public was illegal.

A cop came up to us before we swiped our metro cards and pointed at our beers. I quietly put my beer down on the ground. This is a maneuver that only seems sneaky to an extremely intoxicated person. The cop said 'Are you gonna throw that away?' We walked to the nearest trash cans and threw away our beers. The cop walked in the opposite direction.

Peter and I sat on a bench in the middle of one of the less crowded blocks in midtown Manhattan and I called a phone number, which I had saved

in my phone as 'Drug Dealer'. A man answered the phone whose voice I recognized to be Alex's. He is the boss of ~4 other drug dealers who normally answer. I told him my order and he said he would be there in 5 minutes, which I knew meant he would be there in 15.

He called and told me that he was in the middle of the block and he could see me. I left Peter alone and met Alex across the street. The other drug dealers didn't mind when Peter came with me, but Alex always requested that I leave him behind.

Alex held both of my hands, covertly slipping an envelope full of cocaine and xanax into my right hand as I put a wad of money in his left hand. He kissed my cheek and gave me a hug that was a few seconds too long for our level of familiarity. 'How have you been sweetheart? How's your boyfriend?' I responded 'He's not my boyfriend' because I thought Alex would enjoy hearing that and be more likely to give me free drugs in the future. 'What is he then? A friend with benefits?' I responded 'Yeah, something like that.'

He asked me if I saw the fireworks over the Hudson River and I said I hadn't. He told me that he kayaks on the Hudson sometimes and would like to take me. He took a sharpie out of his pocket

and wrote 'kayaking' on a piece of paper with a phone number. He explained that the number I normally call is the 'business number', but if I want to go kayaking with him, I should call the number he just wrote down. I thanked him and said I would definitely be calling soon.

Peter and I got in a cab headed back to Peter's apartment.

Across the street from Peter's apartment there was a high school under construction.

We noticed that the front gate, which had previously been blocking us from entering the construction area of the high school, was open. We walked up 3 stories of scaffolding.

On the roof we saw fireworks going off in the distance. We had sex with me leaning over the cement wall surrounding the edge of the roof and Peter behind me. I could see Peter's apartment from this position. We finished having sex with me face first on the ground, and Peter on top.

It was 95 degrees and I could feel pieces of dirt and gravel sticking to my body underneath my clothes as we walked down the scaffolding. Peter

walked ahead of me.

When Peter reached the bottom, I heard a male voice say 'Put your hands where I can see them.' Peter put his hands up and a cop pulled him out of my view. I instinctively put my hands above my head. One cop put his hand on the narrow part of my waist and another cop put his hand on my lower back, as they lead me off the scaffolding to the ground, where I saw Peter standing with the third cop, who was holding him by the arm.

The cop said 'I am going to put you in handcuffs now, okay?' in a tone that sounded almost sympathetic or comforting. I said 'okay' and he put Peter and I in handcuffs. The cop took Peter out of my view, while another cop grabbed my purse.

I said 'Are you going to search my bag?' and the cop said 'Are you fucking kidding? You're trespassing on a construction site doing god knows what. Of course I'm going to search your fucking bag. You could have weapons.'

At that point I remembered I had $80 worth of cocaine and ~10-15 illegal fireworks in my purse (Peter had the xanax in his pocket). I remembered my stepdad telling me when I was younger that if I was ever in possession of illegal drugs and a cop

was going to search me, I should say 'I do not consent to this search' because there is a law where cops sometimes can't search you if you say that.

I said 'I do not consent to this search' and the cop paused for a second. He responded 'Look you're obviously doing something illegal, I could take you to jail right now, so don't pull this 'I don't consent' shit with me. Lets not get off on the wrong foot. Now do you wanna start over again?'

'Yes sir. I'm sorry.'

'What the fuck were you doing up there? Is there anything damaged? Any broken windows?'

'No.'

'So what were you doing up there?'

'Honestly we were just exploring, we didn't mean any harm.'

'What the fuck do you mean exploring? What the fuck...are you a prostitute?'

'No, god no. I work full time in the publicity department of a publishing company. We were honestly just looking around.'

The other cop began removing things from my purse. He pulled out a roman candle and a handful of firecrackers. 'What the hell is this, where did you get these?'

'I found them.'

The cop pulled my ID out of my purse and shined his flashlight on it. He said my full name but with the wrong pronunciation. 'My-Ra Gonzalez'.

I stared at him and felt my emotional state change from 'horrified' to 'annoyed' then back to 'horrified'.

The other cop walked Peter toward us, still holding him by the arm. He said 'So, do you guys really want this?' The other two cops looked confused. 'I mean, do you wanna bother with these guys?'

'Oh,' said the cop who was searching my purse. 'Yeah, they aren't worth it. We have better things to do.'